Media depend on people. If you want to create and use media in Christian ministry efficiently and effectively, you need to focus on audiences. Working for and with people assures that audiences can relate the biblical message better to their lived realities. *Translating the Bible into Media* is packed with invaluable information and practical advice about how to create audio and visual media. Its author excels at presenting a wealth of experience that builds on current views of media and communication. This essential book will be most useful for anyone who is interested in Christian media ministry or wishes to train others.

Johannes Merz, PhD
Senior Anthropology Consultant, SIL Global

The publication of this practical book is timely, as many Christian communicators today are grappling with the best way to use the wide range of media available to us. Andreas has opened the door to many different ways of interacting with modern media, while offering advice on choosing the best approach for a particular situation. I highly recommend this book to anyone wanting to harness the potential of communication technologies to communicate and to facilitate holistic development through community driven communication.

Margaret Hill
Senior Translation Consultant, SIL Global

If you want to create effective video or audio content for ministry without spending much time and money, this book is for you. I wish I had this knowledge earlier. After reading the book I went out with my camera to try some of the ideas and came back more satisfied with my work than ever before. *Translating the Bible into Media* is a practical book, inspiring you to use media in ways that facilitate participation and transformation as you give voice to your audience. This not only allows your ministry partners to thrive as they discover and put their gifts to use; it also results in content that is highly relevant to them.

John L. Ommani, PhD
Scripture Engagement Consultant and Trauma Healing Master Facilitator, Africa Area, SIL Global

Media is one of the seven influencers of society identified by YWAM founder, Loren Cunningham. The way we engage with it can further or hinder God's Kingdom. This book is drawn from a rich ministry experience and is suitable to equip individuals, organizations, and communities to harness the potential of media.

Michel Kenmogne, PhD
Executive Director, SIL Global, 2016–2025

Translating the Bible into Media

SIL Global
Publications in Scripture Engagement 3

Publications in Scripture Engagement is a peer-reviewed series published by SIL Global. Using the languages that people understand and identify with can both strengthen the use and impact of the Bible, and help strengthen the use of local languages. While most volumes are authored by members of SIL Global, suitable works by others occasionally form part of the series.

Susan McQuay: Series Editor, Managing Editor
Eleanor McAlpine: Copy Editor
Priscilla Higby: Production Manager
Elke Meier: Compositor
Barbara Alber: Graphic Designer and Cover Designer

Attributions

Three men and a radio page 56, photo by Martin Plüss. Used by permission.
Voice recorder page 109, public domain, CC0 1.0 Universal.
Microphones with polar pattern page 110, adapted by the author from an original image by Jaduial from Pixabay.
Handheld microphone page 110, public domain, CC0 1.0.
Surface microphone page 111, public domain, CC BY-SA 3.0.
Lavalier microphone page 111, public domain, CC0 1.0.
Wireless microphone page 111, photo by Marco Verch, Flickr photo, CC BY 2.0.
Boom microphone page 111, illustration by Lionel Allorge. Wikimedia. CC BY-SA 3.0.
Stand with microphone page 111. OpenClipart-Vectors from Pixabay.
Pop filter page 111, photo by Tim Reckmann, CC BY 2.0 DE.
Headphones page 112, public domain. Photo on Pixnio.
Drawings on pages 122 and 137 used with the kind permission of the estate of Paul White Productions.
Choir page 124, with thanks to Raube Kawtal UEEC Tokombéré.
Musical performance page 125, with thanks to "Groupe Arts et Vision de LANDA-KASSI", Kara, Togo.
3D gray camera man images page 141, image by Peggy und Marco Lachmann-Anke from Pixabay.
DSLR camera page 143, image by Clker-Free-Vector-Images from Pixabay.
3D gray man and mobile phone page 145, image by Peggy und Marco Lachmann-Anke from Pixabay.
Camcorder page 145, CC0 1.0 Universal (CC0 1.0) Public Domain Dedication.
DSLR camera page 145, image by OpenClipart-Vectors from Pixabay.
Action camera page 147, adapted from image by Nils Stawitzki from Pixabay.
Cliparts on page 149, OpenClipart-Vectors from FreeSVG.
Puzzle on page 150, adapted from image by Clker-Free-Vector-Images from Pixabay.
All other photos and illustrations: Copyright © Andreas Ernst. Used by permission.

Translating the Bible into Media
Second Edition

Andreas Ernst

SIL Global
Dallas, Texas

Library of Congress Control Number: 2025945749
ISBN: 978-1-55671-589-1 (pbk)
ISBN: 978-1-55671-590-7 (ePub)
ISSN: 2994-7286

Copyright © 2025 by SIL Global. All rights reserved.
First edition published 2023.

No part of this publication may be reproduced, stored in a retrieval system, or transmitted in any form or by any means—electronic, mechanical, photocopy, recording, or otherwise—without the express permission of SIL Global. However, short passages, generally understood to be within the limits of fair use, may be quoted without permission.

Data and materials collected by researchers in an era before documentation of permission was standardized may be included in this publication. SIL makes diligent efforts to identify and acknowledge sources and to obtain appropriate permissions wherever possible, acting in good faith and on the best information available at the time of publication.

Copies of this and other publications of SIL Global may be obtained through distributors such as Amazon, Barnes & Noble, other worldwide distributors and, for select volumes, publications.sil.org:

SIL Global Publishing Services
7500 W Camp Wisdom Road
Dallas, TX 75236-5629 USA
publications@sil.org

Meaning is not something that is delivered to people, people create/interpret it themselves. Knowledge in society is not objective or static, but is ever changing and infused with the values and realities faced by those who have it.

J. Servaes and P. Malikhao

An onslaught of opinions about what is taking place in the world today comes from every direction: social media, news feeds, popular podcasts, blogs, radio, and television. […] This is quickly becoming one of the fiercest battlegrounds on which we must fight as godly leaders who live and work in an ungodly culture.

J. C. Erlacher

Contents

Foreword   xi

1 Introduction   1
   1.1   Why this book?   1
   1.2   Artificial Intelligence—What are its implications?   3
   1.3   Biblical promises for communicators   5
   1.4   How to teach the content of this book to others   6

2 Understanding Your Audience   9
   2.1   Researching the needs of your audience   9
   2.2   Research methods   12

3 Media Strategies for Social Change   17
   3.1   Six factors that increase the impact of your media   17
        3.1.1   Integrated into media habits   21
        3.1.2   Identification with content   25
        3.1.3   Interactivity   28
        3.1.4   Influence through tangible role models   29
        3.1.5   Involvement   33
        3.1.6   Independence   35
   3.2   *Eyes for Impact*: A visual tool for media planning and assessment   38

4 Understanding Media Platforms   55
   4.1   Radio   56
   4.2   Social media   60
   4.3   Podcasting   63
   4.4   Social gatherings   64
   4.5   Websites   65
   4.6   Television   67

5 Simple and Effective Audio Genres for Ministry 69
    5.1 Different audio genres for different purposes 69
    5.2 Interviews and talk shows 75
    5.3 Debates 77
    5.4 Interactive Bible studies 80
    5.5 Participatory radio drama 81
    5.6 Musical composition and song writing 88
    5.7 Radio spots 91
    5.8 Audio Scriptures 92
    5.9 Audio documentaries 97
    5.10 Apps 101

6 Advice on Audio Recording Equipment 103
    6.1 Understanding sound cards 103
    6.2 Using sound cards for recording scripted content or music 105
    6.3 Recording in dynamic situations 109
    6.4 Understanding microphones 110
    6.5 Additional recording equipment 111
    6.6 Recording sound effects 112

7 Simple and Effective Video Genres for Ministry 115
    7.1 Different videos for different purposes 115
    7.2 Image-based videos 121
    7.3 Music videos 123
    7.4 "Talking head" videos 128
    7.5 Participatory short films 133

8 Video Recording Equipment 143

9 Script Writing 149
    9.1 General principles of script writing 149
    9.2 Four types of scripts 150
    9.3 Researching information for a script 153
    9.4 Intellectual property and copyright 154

10 Conclusion 157

Glossary 159

References 161

Foreword

Mobile phones are everywhere. Thanks to their global popularization, communication and entertainment technologies have reached people and places which were formerly considered unreachable. In fact, one might argue that information communication technologies have become a kind of language of wider communication in themselves. This development presents new opportunities to those who are seeking to communicate God's message of love. While communication technology comes with a new set of challenges and pitfalls, its potential for creating constructive dialogue and positive change is unquestionable.

Have you ever asked yourself the following questions: What does good stewardship of communication technology look like in God's kingdom? What responsibility do we have as communication technology users with regard to people groups that are used to receiving and sharing information through oral communication, but are often marginalized because of their linguistic and educational background?

You can read this book in self-study or use it as a course manual to train others. In either case, its main purpose is to equip those who desire to bring hope to others and inspire transformation through media. The formats and strategies in this book can be used in a variety of contexts. They are designed to keep program and equipment costs low, while capitalizing on local participation and aiming for sustainability. Speaking of sustainability: Technology changes continuously. However, the more we focus on technology, the more restless we can become as we play catch-up with the latest technological solutions and opportunities in our ministry approach. This can distract us from other factors which are far more detrimental when it comes to spiritual transformation and behavioral change. For this reason, this book focuses on universally true media communication principles, alongside equipment criteria and production processes which continue to be valid even as technologies evolve. Yes, new technologies such as AI help to speed up processes, but technology itself can never replace the need for human beings to engage in authentic conversations with other humans, about specific and personal life questions for specific contexts, to find heartfelt and trustworthy wisdom, one day at a time.

You will find ideas here for making use of traditional media services such as radio or TV. However, this book also allows you to develop effective content and programs for communities with limited access to traditional media by using platforms such as social media or listening groups. Whatever your situation is, one thing never changes in communication: If you know your target audience well and are willing to adapt to its realities and interests, new faith conversations will emerge which have the power to change lives.

May God grant you the pleasure of being able to share His wisdom in creative, practical, and powerful ways! And may you grow in experience, so that you can equip many others to transmediate the Word of God into the lives of your audiences, for His glory.

1
Introduction

1.1   Why this book?

Dear Reader,

Imagine, if you will, a conversation between you and me about this book that goes something like this...

You: Why is this book entitled "Translating the Bible into Media"?

A: Technology is at the center of Bible translation, allowing us to create Bible products to bridge the problem of limited access to God's Word. As a result, we easily get more excited about technology than people. Technology is measurable, controllable and efficient, and we can begin to see it as our closest ally in accomplishing God's purposes.

You: I see. I think the correct term for this view of technology is technological optimism, right?

A: Exactly! However, because of this view, we can forget that the people we serve require a kind of love and attention that is more personal and conversational, more sacrificial, and less predictable.

You: Are you saying you are pessimistic about technology?

A: Not at all! But God's Word is not mere information or knowledge. Rather, it serves as a two-directional medium, connecting humans with each other and God through His ongoing story with mankind. Therefore, Bible translation into a given language must always be accompanied by an equally important translation process which mediates God's Word through ordinary people and life experiences, building on the communication preferences, media habits and personal testimony of those who are engaging with it. Communication technologies are simply media. When you mediate something, there is usually a point A and a point B. However, it would be a mistake to think of point B as inferior to point A, or the other way around, otherwise you end up with a broken chain of communication. In the 1970s, communication experts realized that development does not happen when you try to impose ideas on people because you assume all they need is to receive the right information from the technologically advanced. As it turns out, more often than not, such top-down approaches have underestimated the knowledge and wisdom that was already available in a given context. Not only is local knowledge sufficient to solve many of the local problems of development, but it is also the only way of actually defining the problems that matter in that context. The same is largely true today for God's message of love relayed in the Bible. In most contexts, you are not going to bring that message to people in your suitcase or on an audio player. In most cases, the gospel message is already present, with some people accepting it, and others rejecting it. I have found that, in these kinds of situations, media should mainly be used for conversations about the gospel, not simply for bringing the gospel. This means that media needs to champion people. It needs to create a dialogue between local Christians and local audiences in order to talk about how the gospel connects with local realities.

You: I see. Does this mean that for you there is no place for transmitting the Bible in the form of audio Bibles or biblical films because most people already know the gospel?

A: Not quite. I think there will always be a place for content that consists of nothing else than the Scriptures, trusting that God can use it to speak directly to those who are seeking to understand it. Besides, God's Word offers protection from spiritual abuse and false teachings, especially when it is translated into the languages of your audiences. What I am saying is that these days people are saturated with information and, as a result, our audiences have become very selective in their use of the media. To use a biblical metaphor, many good seeds fall among the rocks or on the path. Sadly, the very rise of communication technology means that most audiences are often presented with many contradictory views and recommendations on the issues they face. It is not surprising then, that simply having access to the Bible does not necessarily lead to an understanding of the transformative love of God. As with the seed carried away by the birds, if the Bible is not understood as being relevant to life, it is quickly filtered out in the buzz of daily noise. The Bible tells us in 1 Peter 3:15–16: Always be prepared to give an answer to everyone who asks you to give the reason for the hope that you have. But do this with gentleness and respect, keeping a clear conscience, so that those who speak maliciously against your good behavior in Christ may be ashamed of their slander. In other words, we must set out from a position of respect for others by connecting the Scriptures with their realities. If we are gentle and the hope in us becomes apparent in real life (also referred to as "good behavior" in verse 16), expect there to be questions. This is what this book is about! Many media platforms today either exploit people financially or impoverish them spiritually. People feel this and, although they are often media saturated, they are still searching for trustworthy voices with relevance and meaningful perspectives on the realities they face. How can we demonstrate through media that we are gentle and respectful? How do we model the hope in us in such a way that people are drawn to it and want to start a conversation? If this topic interests you, this book is for you.

You: Ok, thank you! One last question. Why is this book a training manual?

A: This book is a training manual because media ministry is not just about communicating God's Word to others using technology. Often others are in a much better position than we are when it comes to translating God's Word into the realities of a given context. In such situations we still have a role. But rather than being the main communicators, our role becomes equipping others as they translate, or shall I say mediate, God's Word into the lives of others.

You: Thanks for taking the time to chat. How about if we dedicate this book with a prayer?

A: Yes, please!

You: Dear Lord, thank you for how you have demonstrated your love by becoming a human being and walking in our midst. Please help us to use media in the same way, connecting and walking with people through ordinary life. And grant us the discernment to recognize when technology gets in the way or becomes a distraction. Amen.

1.2 Artificial Intelligence—What are its implications?

Undoubtedly, the rise of Artificial Intelligence (AI) has changed the way we communicate. While we are only beginning to understand the potential of AI, perhaps this is a good time to consider some of its implications for Christian ministry. First of all, it can be argued that AI in and of itself is neutral. As with all technologies, it can be used for good or for bad. However, as Lennox points out, because AI relies on the data created by human beings, there is a real danger in AI enforcing the kind of morality, or lack thereof, which is typical of the human condition.[1] For instance, is it ethical to use AI to create avatars of deceased family members so that family members can continue to have daily conversations with them? What sort of worldview lies behind such efforts? In fact, one might be forgiven for asking if there are any ethical considerations at all behind this use of technology, considering the commercial benefits and exploitation it offers. Similarly, as AI and AR (augmented reality) continue to empower the computer games industry, what are we to make of the negative impact of today's gaming culture on different age groups? While AI appears to be neutral, we cannot expect it to have a moral will of its own or be free of moral influence. Rather, we should expect it to continue to enforce the commercial, political and religious exploitation that is typical for the way humans use communication technologies. However, rather than demonizing AI, I believe it is our duty as Christians to continue to monitor how AI marginalizes and exploits people, while at the same time making use of the opportunities it offers. Especially in the domain of content creation, AI offers many exciting solutions.

Translating, subtitling or dubbing videos and films has become easier than ever, and creating podcasts or documentaries can be made more effective using transcription or text-to-audio conversion tools. AI also allows us to create images and animations to suit our communication needs, without the need for strong IT skills. Not surprisingly, there is much excitement about AI and the many benefits it promises in reaching audiences with the gospel. However, the opportunities provided by AI raise a new set of ethical questions: When using automated content adaption or creation processes, how relevant to the audience is the content we are adapting, and is there a risk of "exporting" Western values or interpretations of the gospel? How do we ensure that automated processes are accompanied by checking processes such as audience testing or back translation? How might AI exacerbate the dominance of the English language, and any worldviews related to it, over communities whose knowledge and realities are not represented in its database? Do we let efficient content creation procedures get in the way of local participation and ownership, and the contextualization of the gospel, or can we harness them to empower the people we serve? Do we miss out on the transformative power of social learning as we bypass authentic conversations with local believers?

In conclusion, while AI offers many tools for more effective content creation, translating the Bible into media will always depend on human intelligence and moral choices. Ultimately, it is through the personal involvement and collaboration of human beings in specific cultures and places that AI can find useful application, while minimizing its tendency to marginalize and exploit. In fact, with the blurring of the boundaries between reality and artificial reality, and the resulting lack of trust towards media, I believe human agency and audience participation will only gain in importance in communicating the gospel in the years to come.

---

1 Lennox 2020.

1.3 Biblical promises for communicators

Before we get into the juicy bits about different media strategies, formats, and equipment, let's remember what it's all about: We are called to be light and salt in this world. This is not an optional activity that we may get interested in or not; it should be part of our very identity and calling. What this means is that God has already prepared good works for us to do, works of shining His light, of communicating His hope. You may feel overwhelmed by the very thought of using new technologies, but don't be discouraged. Let the following ten biblical principles and promises be an encouragement to you. Each starts with one of the letters of the words APPLY TRUTH:

- **All languages**. God's message must be communicated in all languages: Acts 2:4, 7-11; Revelation 7:9; John 19:19-22.
- **Promised impact**. Not everyone will engage with the message, but communicating God's message of love will be fruitful: 2 Timothy 4:2-4; Isaiah 55:11; 2 Corinthians 2:14-17; Matthew 13:4-23.
- **Practical**. The message needs to connect with reality. How can we help people understand how to apply the Bible to their lives in a concrete way?: Matthew 28:19-20; Matthew 7:15-20; James 1:23-27.
- **Living example**. The way we live our lives must match the message: James 2:14-19; 1 Peter 2:15.
- **Youth**. Children and young people are in a stage of life where they are learning a lot about the world and life: Matthew 19:14; Ecclesiastes 12:1.
- **Thought penetration**. Our responsibility is to penetrate the thinking (understanding) of those who listen to our media: Matthew 13:18-19; 2 Corinthians 10:5; Romans 12:2.
- **Record it**. It is good to save God's words (to record them) so that the message may remain trustworthy, authoritative, and always accessible: Jeremiah 36:1-3; 2 Chronicles 34:14-21.
- **Under God's control**. Let us not have confidence in our own eloquence, seek our own glory, or be intimidated by professional actors, musicians, or commentators! 1 Corinthians 1:17-18, 26-27; John 6:44; 1 Timothy 2:1-4.
- **Take the opportunity**. Look for opportunities to connect with our audiences on their terms, including with the use of technology: 1 Corinthians 9:19-23; Romans 10:17; Acts 17:22-27; 2 Thessalonians 2:15; Ecclesiastes 11:4-6.
- **Heartfelt understanding**. Use testimonies (Matthew 5:15-16; 1 Peter 3:15-16; Luke 8:39; 1 Corinthians 10:1-6, 11), stories (Matthew 13:10-15; 2 Samuel 12:1-9), drama (Jeremiah 19:1-4, 10-11) as well as songs and dances (Psalm 147:7; Ephesians 5:18-19; Psalm 150:3-5; Deuteronomy 31:19-21) to present a memorable message.

1.4 How to teach the content of this book to others

You may want to cover only parts of this book with your students, but here is how you can systematically cover all of its content using two workshops, each lasting two weeks:

Workshop I: Media Strategies and Audio Production	
Day 1	Biblical promises for communicators, Overview of audio genres Recording equipment
Day 2	Understanding your audience, Research methods and assignment Audacity*: Basic recording and editing
Day 3	Six factors for effective communication and social change Audacity: More advanced skills
Day 4	Sound effects, Understanding different media platforms Audacity: Multitrack editing, creating a radio spot (Project 1)
Day 5	Script writing, How to record Scriptures Scripture-recording project (Project 2)
Day 6	Project 2 continued Participatory Radio Drama: Creating a drama as a class
Day 7	Editing and completing a radio drama edit (Project 3) Copyright and intellectual property
Day 8	Conducting interviews and group facilitation Preparing a debate, followed by recording a debate
Day 9	How to create a documentary (Project 4) Project 4: Conducting interviews on the streets for the documentary project
Day 10	Documentary project: Editing Completing all projects, Instructions for post-course project

* Audacity is a highly popular open-source audio editing software which offers many different interface languages. Using this type of free software allows partners around the world to create content without depending on online payment methods and financial means that may not be available to them.

Workshop II: Media Strategies and Video Production	
Day 1	Creating videos from still images (Project 1) Overview of video genres
Day 2	Completing Project 1, Video recording equipment Shot types and camera movements Participatory film development (HEARD approach)—Demo
Day 3	Preparing a film script, Directing a scene Demonstration of directing and recording scene 1
Day 4	Editing a scene (video editing foundations) Preparing assigned scenes in groups (Project 2), Shoot scenes 2 and 3
Day 5	Advanced editing of a scene Shoot scenes 4 and 5, Edit scenes over the weekend
Day 6	Review edited scenes, Music videos, Music recording Live demo of recording a musical composition
Day 7	Editing a music mix, How to edit a music video (Project 3) Preparing a music video recording (assigning tasks) Live demo of recording a music video
Day 8	Advanced music video editing, How to record an interview Informational video (Project 4): Students record interviews and footage for their project
Day 9	Complete projects
Day 10	Complete projects, Instructions for post-course project

2
Understanding Your Audience

> Our culture obsesses over numbers. We quantify success as the number of clients or sales, miles run, or likes on social media....The urgency to measure success even infiltrates the church. While there are some great reasons for measuring, it can also be a distraction. Scriptures show us again and again that God does not measure success in numbers. If anything, the opposite is true. God receives glory when he uses the one or the few and the most unlikely.[2]
>
> *Jolene Cassellius Erlacher*

> Simply getting more people to be aware of you is not going to help you accomplish your bigger organizational goals. Getting more people to hear your voice does not necessarily mean that more people will listen.[3]
>
> *Julia Campbell*

2.1 Researching the needs of your audience

Before developing any kind of media product or program, you need to be interested in how your message or content might meet the specific needs of the people you have in mind. This means you cannot group people into

---

2   Erlacher 2018:loc 1764.
3   Campbell 2020:loc 421.

target audiences which fit generalized, measurable criteria such as all speakers of a certain language, or everyone living in a specific location. Every community consists of a number of subgroups, all of which have their own specific needs and media habits. We must therefore assume that, while we may want to bring hope to everyone in a community, doing this practically speaking requires that we identify and seek to understand a number of subgroups in this community. I will cover the topic of identifying your target audience more in detail later, but, generally speaking, understanding the issues people are dealing with in a community helps us identify the media content this community will appreciate. However, identifying appropriate topics is not enough. To cover the issues your target audiences face in a way that is helpful to them, you also want to understand the causes of local problems, how these problems impact the lives of the community or its subgroups, and what kinds of solutions the community itself has to offer to address such issues.

When you see the needs of a community as challenges which have local solutions, this allows you as a communicator to bring hope to the community and empower community members who are able to offer help or know-how. Of course, not all problems can be solved using only local resources, but as Christian communicators, we want to emphasize that God is already at work in the community and is more than able to bring fruit from the little we have to offer as human beings. This is particularly true because almost all issues your target audiences face have a practical as well as a spiritual component. For example, while secular aid organizations tend to focus on overcoming issues related to the physical wellbeing of a community such as alcoholism or unemployment, as Christian communicators we must also seek to understand and address the spiritual needs that lie at the root of these. Our role as communicators is therefore holistic. On the one hand, we are called to offer spiritual answers, which first of all means giving voice to local people who are able to provide spiritual advice to others living in the community. On the other hand, we are also called to offer practical help (James 2:14-19), which means identifying and giving voice to a number of people who have practical help to offer. Spiritual and practical needs are strongly interconnected with one another:

> The effect of only witnessing to the spiritual truth of the gospel is a serious distortion of the gospel. In response to hearing the gospel only as word addressing spiritual need, people may experience only a conversion at the level of formal religion and begin to go to church, read their Bible, and identify themselves as Christians. Yet, the other two dimensions of their worldview remain untouched by the gospel.[4]
>
> *Bryant Myers*

---

4   Myers 2011:loc 6881.

While spritual and practical (physical) needs are strongly interconnected, it can be helpful to identify specific problems in a given context and try to make sense of them in terms of underlying physical and spiritual needs. Here are a few examples of problems found in many communities, which may be strongly connected either with spiritual needs or physical needs. As you read through these examples, you will quickly see that it is impossible to overcome all of the problems in a given context without offering both practical as well as spiritual help:

- **Spiritual needs**: Behaviors such as adultery, witchcraft, alcoholism, domestic violence, suspicion of one another, arguments, jealousy, pornography, neglect of children or responsibilities, laziness, thievery, and many other problems related to moral conduct show us the spiritual needs of a community. Researching spiritual needs such as these and the assumptions or worldviews that cause them allows you to understand the underlying mental and spiritual barriers that need overcoming so people can be free to overcome the physical challenges in their environment.
- **Practical needs**: Poverty, water shortage, illnesses, lack of food, infertile land, unemployment, lack of schooling, and many other problems related to practical living are often caused by poverty, political instability, economic exploitation, and the lack of infrastructure, information, or adequate education. Understanding practical needs such as these allows you to offer media content to your audiences which provides advice and support on practical issues such as health, agriculture, and human rights. Such programs demonstrate true care and love, and establish a basis of trust for talking about deeper spiritual issues.

> To use aid to promote a particular religion is not appropriate, they say. And, of course, they are right. Any Christian would agree. But Western governments go a step further and make a bad mistake. In the name of separation of church and state, a logical extension of the modern separation of the spiritual and the material, they require that the programming they fund can never include anything remotely religious in nature. This demand for purely materialistic programming is at complete odds with the holistic worldview of most of the people who are the recipients of development aid.[5]
>
> *Bryant Myers*

---

5   Myers 2011:loc 6956.

2.2 Research methods

There are different ways to research your audience's needs. The approach you choose will depend on your relationship to the community and the amount of time you are willing to invest. However, no matter what limitations and opportunities you face, it is always a good idea to use more than one approach in order to understand the needs of your audience more accurately and make sure you understand the specific needs of its subgroups. I also highly recommend getting people involved in your research who understand the local culture and language and whose presence in the community is less likely to influence your results. Regardless of how you go about it, researching your audience is an ongoing process that needs to be repeated on a regular basis. As with all relationships, the more you know your audience, the more you will love them and the more they will love and trust you.

Focus groups

One of the best ways to research the needs of a community is to organize homogenous groups for discussing local issues. These are groups of people that share a common identity such as belonging to the same age group, gender, social class, professional community, or sharing the same traditional or religious role, or the same level of education. With the help of some key questions, it is easy to launch a discussion between  members of such a group because nobody feels inferior to the others or that they are misunderstood. Consequently, all you need to do is to listen carefully to the points of view, problems, and solutions brought forth by the group in order to find out some of the community's needs as well as how these could be addressed. The more different focus groups you hold discussions with, the more you will understand the needs of the community as a whole.

Observation

By observing the behavior and conversations of people (for example, during local events such as market activities, festivals, or ceremonies, as well as in conflict situations and private or public discussions) one can get valuable insights into the needs of a community. This approach is particularly helpful considering that what people say doesn't always reflect what they really believe, while behavior is a good demonstration of deeply rooted beliefs and values. It is also worth observing what people don't do or talk about, such as the lack of interaction with HIV-infected members of the community or talking about sexuality. Writing down your observations can help you remember and think more about the needs of a community in order to understand them. In this way, you can identify the causes and their impact, and consider possible solutions.

Interviews with key people

In order to find out about the problems of a community you can interview the community leaders such as teachers, church leaders and other clergy, or even politicians. These people often see the needs in the practical life of the community as their work involves providing help in the community. Church leaders can often point out the spiritual needs of the community. However, church leaders are often appointed from outside the community. This means that, while they may  provide more objective insights, their understanding of the community can be limited. In this case, you may also want to interview church elders. In addition, it is also good to interview people from the lowest class in the community as they often give us more concrete information about the practical problems the community faces daily. It is a good idea to prepare some key questions before doing your interviews and communicate them to the interviewees beforehand so that you and the interviewees can prepare yourselves. To understand the needs of your target community even better, ask your interviewees to share testimonies or give examples of the kinds of issues they consider noteworthy. It can also be helpful to record your interviews as this will give you more time later to analyze what was said.

Surveys

To obtain more statistical information on specific issues, it can be useful to carry out a survey or opinion poll in a community. While surveys are used to collect information or the opinion of a greater number of people, you must limit your questions to very specific information, facts, or opinions that are easy to process and compare later such as, "Do you own a smart phone?", "How many times do you use the internet per week?", or "Out of ten school dropouts in this town, how many do you think are unemployed?" Written surveys can give participants more time to reflect and answer, but only if you are targeting a part of the population that has sufficient writing skills. In communities where few people can read, ask your questions orally and take notes for yourself.

Participation in content creation

One of the most effective research methods is to get your audience involved in creating content for themselves. By using formats such as debates, documentaries, participatory radio drama, or interactive Bible studies, you do not have to know much about the target audience to start with. Instead, your role as media specialist is to give voice to others and learn about their needs and views as you facilitate and observe participants throughout the content creation process.

Developing audience profiles

Before developing a media strategy for a particular community, it is important to understand more specifically what kinds of people within a given community you want to connect with. In fact, if you decide that you want to reach everyone in a community, you run the risk of reaching no one at all. A good communicator wants to know the following: How would I describe a typical member of my target audience? What is their age or educational background? What profession or social rank is typical for such a person? What specific challenges does this person face, and what are their interests and habits in terms of the use of communication technology? Once you have thought through these questions, you can start to develop an effective media strategy to connect and stay in

Audience Profile

Typical/average age:
Gender (if gender specific):
Typical marital status:
Typical level of education:
Typical occupations/professions:
Frequently visited places, events:

Social status and role:
Frequently encountered difficulties:
Areas of interests: professional & daily life
Media habits: Preferred platforms and audio-visual content, time (of the day) spent on them
Religious attitudes:

touch with your target audience. As you develop your audience profile, you may come to realize the need for different media strategies to reach different target audiences.

On page 14 you see an example of an audience profile form, which can help you deepen your understanding of your target audience(s).

To conclude this section, I'd like to draw your attention to one more delicate matter. As outside ministry or aid specialists, we often go about analyzing the needs of those we are serving through conversations with them. This has great value and shows much needed respect and humility. However, what we often forget is that local partners themselves don't naturally understand the needs of their own community, not least because any given person can only truly be a part of a very narrow subgroup within a community. As a result, we do well as communicators to help local partners assess both the physical and spiritual needs of their own community and its subgroups for themselves.

3
Media Strategies for Social Change

One of the dangers of audiovisual production is to become so focused on creating content that is technically polished, that we forget to connect in meaningful ways with target audiences. We must however keep in mind that audiovisual products by themselves do not automatically lead to change. Communication is highly complex and influenced by many factors. For example, in addition to the purely technical aspects of media, we must understand other aspects of communication: Who should be communicating? What should communication be about? Who decides what needs to be communicated? How does access to information lead to behavioral change, if at all? Who makes the choices about the right technologies to choose? All of these questions also raise questions about the role of international ministry organizations in cross-cultural contexts: Should we act as outside technology providers, or are we to actively pursue collaboration with local communities, learning from one another? How can we get an accurate understanding of the technology and communication needs of the people we are hoping to reach or serve?

3.1 Six factors that increase the impact of your media

As you assess or begin to develop new media strategies for reaching a given community, I encourage you to think about six major impact factors which I believe to be foundational in reaching your audience effectively.

In this section we will look at the theory behind each of these six impact factors. In section 3.2 we will then get to know a visualized participatory planning tool called *Eyes for Impact*, which, based on six impact questions, allows you to assess, revise or develop new media strategies for reaching your audience.

> **Integrated** into media habits:
> Are you using the right media platforms the right way and at the right time?
>
> **Identification** with content:
> Does your content appeal to your audience in terms of their interests and preferences?
>
> **Interactivity**:
> Can your audience interact with your content and with others in order to find purpose and identity?
>
> **Influence**:
> Who influences your audience? What role-models will your audience identify with and learn from?
>
> **Involvement**:
> Does your content or approach encourage beneficiaries to contribute towards and be involved in all steps of the process?
>
> **Independence**:
> Are you intentionally working towards ownership and sustainability?

Before we look at each of the six impact factors, it is important to understand that media is more than the transfer of information from A to B using some form of information communication technology or other. Rather, developing effective media strategies also means taking into account the complex environment of cross-cultural collaboration in which media ministry takes place today. This means that any given media strategy must make sense of and attempt to harmonize a whole range of contributions, technologies, worldviews, and expectations brought to the table by different stakeholders. One such expectation is to do with how we define impact and how we expect to measure it. And this has implications for how we develop media strategies.

As anyone who has been involved in Christian ministry knows, kingdom work can be slow and often discouraging. We often have no harvest where we have sown. For instance, our work often depends on partnerships with financial donors, who are keen on hearing impact stories or expect reports on progress made specifically in the ministry they are giving towards. Particularly when it comes to partner organizations or individuals which provide significant financial support, the desire to justify continued giving and prayer support through measurable outcomes is a constant reality. This may be because of expected reporting procedures, or simply because we feel the need to validate our ministry. Measurable outcomes may take the form of statistical growth in the number of clicks, content downloads, churches planted, Bible study groups created or with regards to the number of completed ministry activities. As missiologist Bessenecker points out, measuring our media impact in this way is problematic:

> [When we succumb to measuring the mission of God solely by these metrics, we succumb to the principalities of profit and miss true signs of kingdom health.]

> The increase of Christ's government and peace defy the easy metrics of the business world, which the church often translates into number of baptisms, congregants and churches, or the size of annual budgets, staff or the number of people served through various ministries. These numbers may provide some helpful information, but they are flimsy indicators of Christ's reign. And when we succumb to measuring the mission of God solely by these metrics, we succumb to the principalities of profit and miss true signs of kingdom health.[6]
>
> Scott A. Bessenecker

The trend towards measurable impact affects how we plan activities and publications in Christian ministry. In fact, we can become so focused on creating polished media content for a given audience or boosting the statistical reach of this content, that we forget to collaborate with the beneficiaries of the content at every stage of the publication and communication process. Sadly, this leads to communication processes which are at best ineffective, and in some cases harmful. Servaes and Malikhao provide the reason for this:

> Meaning is not something that is delivered to people, people create/interpret it themselves. Knowledge in society is not objective or static, but is ever changing and infused with the values and realities faced by those who have it.[7]
>
> Jan Servaes and Patchanee Malikhao

Publishing Christian content or running a number of educational activities for a given community does not automatically lead to change. What leads to change is authentic and ongoing collaboration and dialogue with local partners and individuals. This ensures that our communication efforts and media content address real needs and offer realistic and practical advice given local realities and worldviews. Only in this way can God's truth reach and transform the lives of individuals and communities from within. This means that participatory methods need to become the foundation upon which all media ministry activities are built. Respect for the ability of local partners to not only participate in but also drive social change is therefore foundational to any cross-cultural ministry.

[**Meaning is not something that is delivered to people, people create/interpret it themselves.**]

---

6 Bessenecker 2014.
7 Servaes and Malikhao 2007:175.

Interestingly, there is a lot we can learn about participatory methods through how these methods evolved over the years. In the 1970s top-down models of development began to be officially recognized by social scientists and development practitioners as

not only ineffective but counterproductive. As a result, the involvement and ownership of social change by the beneficiaries themselves took center stage, and a number of participatory methods were developed to foster ownership. More specifically, De Campos (2009) notes how historically participatory methods originated with Rapid Rural Appraisal (RRA), which saw communities as more passive information providers, in order to render development efforts more efficient. He then contrasts this approach with the emergence of Participatory Rural Appraisal (PRA), which emphasized participatory methods as a way to empower communities as the main agents of change for themselves.

We do not have time here to cover the many different forms and interpretations of different participatory methods and processes in detail. However, it is important to remember that what lies at the heart of participatory methods is ownership and contextualization. Both of these goals are far more instrumental in creating lasting social change than efficiency in the planning process, or measurable outcomes. In his landmark book, *Walking with the Poor*, Development Researcher Myers points out just how important it is for Christians to move away from a problem-solving mentality towards a participatory approach in ministry:

> Development practice traditionally began with identifying the community's needs or a needs analysis. Rooted in a problem-solving approach, the task is to identify what is not working or is absent and plan to remedy the problem. This approach has some weaknesses. First, it sees the poor community as a place full of problems, a negative point of departure. While this is understandable for those of us who tend to be a little messianic and see ourselves as God's problem solvers, it tends to obscure the importance of looking for what works and what brings life. [...] A truly Christian approach to designing a transformational development program also needs to be open and attentive to what God has to say to us. Even more important, the community needs to be invited to be open and attentive to what God has to say to it. Together we need to be quiet and listen in the midst of the all the information we have gathered and be open to God leading us to the information and conclusions that God deems most important.[8]
>
> *Bryant Myers*

---

8   Myers 2011:loc 5146–5153.

In other words, Christian ministry has a lot to learn from the participatory approach to social change recommended by community development experts. Taking this approach not only makes sense from a pragmatic point of view; at an even deeper level, our faith commitment and identity define our relationship with the communities we serve as one of mutual accountability and united submission under God's guidance. We must therefore learn to  listen well, both to the people we serve and, together with them, also to God.

It is worth noting here that using participatory methods does not mean harmonious collaboration and fair and egalitarian representation of a given community's needs. In reality, most, if not all, communities we serve consist of a number of subgroups, individuals, and leadership levels with conflicting interests, different worldviews and educational backgrounds. Because of such internal differences, most communities are at best loosely held together by rather dysfunctional decision-making processes. In addition, individuals and subgroups in a community often have very different levels of understanding of what social change is desirable or possible. In addition, many communities are characterized by power hierarchies which are often culturally acceptable, religiously founded or centered around influential people, due to political, financial or spiritual power. Such people often have little genuine interest in communal development and wellbeing. Sadly, such realities are often found in church structures, mirroring more or less what happens in society. Keeping all this in mind, using participatory planning methods in Christian ministry is not about achieving perfect cohesion between all stakeholders. It is however about providing an opportunity for dialogue, and learning together with those who are willing and able to be part of the conversation. Again, as Christians we are called not only to use participatory methods to improve social structures and collaboration; our faith also allows us to see and overcome some of the spiritual realities and barriers we face in a given context.

Having identified participatory approaches as the basis for effective media ministry, let's now discover what this means specifically in terms of the six impact factors.

3.1.1 Integrated into media habits

Media research has shown that the overload of information due to the spread of information and communications technology (ICTs) increasingly leads people to limit their media intake to the kinds of media which satisfy their felt needs. This phenomenon

> By first understanding the media behavior and habits of our audience, we are in a better position to create the right content for the right platform.

has been described under the term UGT, short for "Uses and Gratifications Theory".[9] The same selective media behavior can be seen in how media technologies are adopted: "Simply because a new media device or platform has become available is no guarantee that many people will go on to actually use it" (Vokes 2017). In other words, we cannot assume that our content will automatically be accessed simply because technologically speaking it is now available. In fact, as we will see later, even if it is being liked, clicked on or shared, this is still no guarantee for impact. However, before we can begin to talk about how our content may or may not change lives, we must ask ourselves: How can we effectively reach our audiences despite their selective media habits? The answer lies in adapting to the communication habits of our audience:

> In the attention economy, no one owes you their attention, you have to earn it. Attention cannot be purchased the same way that it could five, 10, 20 years ago, when we had a handful of TV channels to entertain us. [...] It's not the 1950s and you cannot Don Draper yourself to success by yelling at strangers via billboards, purchased email lists, random mailings, and the like. Manipulating people and tricking them into spending their most precious resource—attention—does not lead to trust, and won't result in long-term marketing success.[10]
>
> Julia Campbell

As Picard puts it, "most people have media habits that are fairly stable as long as they meet the individual's needs and wants. These habits save time" (2000). The big question therefore is how to become a part of the already existing media habits of our audience. What platforms do our audience already use, and for what purpose? What type of content is needed to gain and maintain the interest of our audience considering these media habits? We often create media content for our target audience first, and then look for ways to distribute this content. However, as we discover the communication channels and content preferences that are already in place, we realize that our audiences are not likely going to give up their existing habits just because we have some new content to offer in their mother tongue. Rather, our content needs to be tailor-made for the media

---

9   For more information about the UGT, see Ruggiero 2000.
10 Campbell 2020:loc 940.

habits of our audiences: Does my audience tend to listen to radio or learn and educate others through face-to-face conversations? Does it watch TV or is it more likely to be on social media? When during the day or week does my target audience use one or more of these platforms and who else is involved? Does my audience have access to the internet? How does it use cell phones (mobile phones) and what types of phones does it use? How frequently does it use such communication forms or technologies? By first understanding the media behavior and habits of our audience, we are in a better position to create the right content for the right platform. Doing so is not an optional, clever communication trick. It is quite simply the only way to reach our audience effectively. Sometimes we hear statements about the rapid spread of technology and how easy it has become to reach anyone anywhere. However, in reality quite the opposite is true. The more technology-saturated we get, the more our media filters kick in to protect ourselves from information overload. This is a challenge that is not about to go away.

Another reason why we can no longer be satisfied with simply "getting our content out there' is to do with the difference between information and transformation. I think we can all agree that simply receiving information does not automatically change the way we think or act. From a ministry perspective, Jones puts it like this:

> Jesus didn't tell us just to reach nations; he told us to teach nations. Reaching is passive and doesn't require much effort beyond being seen. Teaching, however, requires capturing attention and fostering conversation.[11]
>
> Nona Jones

In other words, understanding the media habits of the people we serve has to do with conversations. Conversations, on the other hand, have to do with regularity and continuity. As we come to understand the role of media habits in shaping the beliefs

---

11 Jones 2020:27 (loc 445).

and behavior of our target audience, we will soon realize that creating one or two one-time products for our audience does not really allow us to sufficiently earn their attention, never mind having a conversation with them. There are many other media channels and platforms out there which put out content on a much more regular basis than we will ever be able to. Many of these channels are more engaging for our audience because of their regularity and conversational nature. Publishing an app in a given language, for example, will not suddenly lead to people regularly using apps or engaging with us about faith topics. Users may download it once and find it exciting. However, if their media habits consists of talking to others, listening to radio or chatting via WhatsApp or Facebook Messenger, you will need to use additional communication forms or content which will keep your audience interested and engaged.

Don't get me wrong. Tools such as audio Bibles and Bible apps have an important place in Christian media, but they need to be embedded in the media habits of users. To achieve this, Bible products need to be used in an environment of regular interaction, which includes regular content output, in order to earn the attention of your audience, grow your listenership/viewership over time as well as promote meaningful engagement. If, for example, your main audience for your Bible app listens to radio on a regular basis or uses Facebook, why not start a Facebook conversation based on the app or hold a weekly radio quiz show which encourages listeners to find answers in the app? Connecting to your audience in this way on their terms is likely going to be far more effective than assuming the app will change lives by mere download.

> **The more technology saturated we get, the more selective our mental media filters get in order to protect ourselves from information overload. This is a challenge that is not about to go away.**

As we realize that keeping conversations going is key to becoming a part of the media habit of our audiences, this not only helps us create the right kind of new content. It also helps us improve our existing content. For example, say you want to use a Bible app alongside a Bible discussion group on radio or Facebook. This may inspire you to add the corresponding Bible study references and questions to your app, so that your audience can read the upcoming questions ahead of time in order to prepare their own personal responses, testimonies or follow-up questions. This may even encourage them to call the radio during the next live Bible study to share their views.

One final observation: More than anything else, social belonging and learning are the most influential factors when it comes to shaping our media habits. As human beings we have a deeply rooted need to learn from and follow others we trust. We also have a strong need to belong to social groups in which our own perspectives are also heard and appreciated. This is why, as we will see soon, interactivity is one of the main impact factors for effective media programs. However, let's first look at the impact factor *Identification with content*. This factor is closely related to *Integrated into media habits*. It looks at content design questions to ensure we are not only reaching our audiences, but doing so in a way that is appealing to them.

3.1.2 Identification with content

Another factor that influences our media ministry impact has to do with the design of our content. The first point to consider when designing content is choosing topics which are of interest to your audience. This can be challenging, given the objectives of Christian ministry. Holistic development and spiritual growth are not always on everyone's agenda, nor are they always a felt need. Quite the opposite: Narcissism and meaningless entertainment and distractions are increasingly numbing the minds of media consumers. Nevertheless, it is possible to let God's transformational principles come alive through the everyday needs and interests of our audiences. In fact, building rapport with audiences through their daily realities not only allows us to meaningfully capture their interest; it also forms the basis upon which God becomes truly tangible and personal in their lives. Myers warns us of the "tendency of some Christians to assume that, since the

Bible is about spiritual things, then the domain to which the Bible speaks is only the spiritual realm. [...] While this is good and proper, it unwittingly precludes the Bible from speaking to the material world of science and development" (2011:loc 6639).

What can we learn from this? Just as every aspect of life ultimately needs God's presence and transformation, the daily life experiences of our audiences can become mirrors or vehicles for reflecting and transmitting his nature and identity to them. Jesus drew his disciples' attention towards the birds and flowers by the roadside in order to teach them important life lessons. In the same way, we need to learn to talk about the things our audiences experience and care about, in order to start conversations with them about God's presence in their lives. We may be tempted to separate spiritual needs from physical needs when it comes to ministry objectives, but as a result we may actually weaken the tangibility of God's presence and love in the lives of our audience. The opposite is also true. As well-known *Times* columnist Matthew Parris, an atheist, concludes about the role of Christian faith in human wellbeing:

> As an atheist I truly believe that Africa needs God: missionaries, not aid money, are the solution to Africa's biggest problem – the crushing passivity of the people's mindset. [...] Travelling in Malawi refreshed another belief, too: one I've been trying to banish all my life, but an observation I've been unable to avoid since my African childhood. It confounds my ideological beliefs, stubbornly refuses to fit my world view, and has embarrassed my growing belief that there is no God. Now a confirmed atheist, I've become convinced of the enormous contribution that Christian evangelism makes in Africa: sharply distinct from the work of secular NGOs, government projects and international aid efforts. These alone will not do. Education and training alone will not do. In Africa Christianity changes people's hearts. It brings a spiritual transformation. The rebirth is real.[12]
>
> *Matthew Parris*

Regardless of whether our audience is interested in agriculture, learning languages, becoming familiar with their political rights, getting to know the Scriptures, how to use pesticides, how to protect themselves from AIDS, how to obtain safe drinking water or how to respond to corruption in the school system, we must ask ourselves whether our ministry activities and content build on the interests of our audience.

Choosing the right topics to cover also requires taking into account other content-related factors such as the religious background and language preferences of our audience, their freedom to engage with a given topic and their worldview and educational background. All of these factors will help us assess what topics can be discussed and at what level.

Making sure our audiences identify with our content also has to do with their learning preferences. If your content is already informed by the *Integrated into media habits* factor, you will probably already know how to at least get your audience's attention. However, content choices such as language choices, communication genres and styles, as well as technical aspects or design aesthetics can further boost the appeal of your content. The choice of appropriate illustrations, font sizes and style, colors, print quality, music and sound effects, etc., are just as important as considering

---

12 Parris 2008, cited in Lennox 2024:114.

literacy or phone literacy levels. In addition, religious and cultural values may determine who can offer advice on what issue, which topics are taboo, or what languages or music styles are appropriate for what purpose. While some audiences like entertainment-based audiovisual content, others may prefer written information presented in a factual way, at least when it comes to certain types of information.

One more observation about content: In Christian ministry we tend to think of media content as Bible-based teaching, information, or conversation. Thinking of media in this way limits the scope of our impact. Media also plays a role in making a ministry or organization known, in raising funds, drawing awareness, promoting buy-in or mobilizing prayer support. These too are important aspects to consider when it comes to content choices which our audiences can relate to. In fact, thinking of media in such broad terms can help us not only deepen our understanding of the topics that need to be covered, but also help us identify new audiences that should be reached in a given ministry.

It is important to note that the two questions *Integrated into media habits?* and *Identification with content?* are very closely interconnected. For instance, content design needs to be adapted to the media habits of the end users. If, for example, you find that your content will mostly likely be listened to by small groups of people rather than individuals, or during rush hour with lots of ambient noise, this has implications for the design of your content. Here's another example: Say you are planning to share Bible-story videos via YouTube because you find out that your audience is regularly on YouTube. However, as you dig deeper into the *Identification with content* factor, you may realize your audience loves music videos and prefers low resolution videos because they listen to these videos with others at work, rather than watching them. The reason may be that only some audience members can afford to buy data, and no one has time to look at the screen anyway. However, as you ask *Identification with content?* questions, you may find out that this group watches these videos in this way for social identification purposes. You may find out that a particular kind of music video is preferred, because it reinforces the religious identity of the group, perhaps even to set itself apart from others at the workplace. How would you go about engaging this audience with this new information in mind? Whatever your approach may be, your *Identification with content?* questions will need to be complemented by insights from your *Integrated into media habits?* questions.

3.1.3 Interactivity

If your content allows listeners and viewers to actively engage in conversations about topics of interest, they are far more likely to engage with it, share it with others and regularly engage with your media on a personal, transformational level. Interactivity creates trust and a sense of belonging to a social group. This in turn leads to real openness towards the views and advice of others, because humans are fundamentally social beings. We do not simply adopt ideas on the basis of logic. And we certainly don't change our habits simply because we have received new information, no matter how convincing this information may be. Rather, new information or ideas are first checked against what others think and recommend. In his seminal work *Diffusion of Innovations*, Everett Rogers describes the social learning process as follows:

> Communication is a process in which participants create and share information with one another in order to reach a mutual understanding. This definition implies that communication is a process of convergence (or divergence) as two or more individuals exchange information in order to move toward each other (or apart) in the meanings that they give to certain events. We think of communication as a two-way process of convergence, rather than as a one-way, linear act in which one individual seeks to transfer a message to another in order to achieve certain effects.[13]
>
> *Everett M. Rogers*

One of the main questions to ask about your ministry activity or content is therefore: Does it invite, or at least allow, end users to express their views, ask questions or comment on the views of others? Does it allow you to engage with the end users and/or allow the end users to engage with one another through ongoing conversations?

Interactivity can be promoted either as an integral part of a content, or, preferably, in terms of how the content is being used in actual conversations. Integrated interactivity can, for example, be found in audio- or text-based content which include written or recorded questions for reflection. Another example of integrated interactivity can be seen with apps that contain games or allow you to share a verse of the day

---

13 Rogers 2010:17.

via social media. However, one should explore whether such integrated interactivity actually leads to real dialogue with others, or simply offers a quirky feature which practically speaking doesn't create any authentic conversations. While building interactivity directly into your content can prove to be difficult, interactive content such as recorded Bible study discussions, talk shows or debates can offer plenty of interactivity and social leaning, which may lead to more social interaction among listeners. However, remember that to promote truly meaningful social interaction which can lead to life changing conversations, your audience needs to be able to join the conversation themselves. This is why interactivity is best promoted in the way a media platform is being used, rather than building some level of interactivity into your content. For example, sharing a simple Bible-story video in a WhatsApp group and launching a conversation about it promises to be far more effective than including a few reflection questions in the video and then uploading it to YouTube.

In addition to building interactivity into your content or promoting conversations around your content, some content allows you to encourage interactivity at a much earlier stage. Participatory radio drama, short film development, or interactive genres such as debates or talk shows not only offer the possibility for continued interactivity in the way they are broadcast or used; they also offer interactivity as part of the content development process itself, meaning participants are given a very authentic opportunity for interacting with others and expressing themselves about the issues they care about most.

To end this section, it is important to remember that the kind of fruitful social interactivity and learning we are seeking to promote is only possible if your audience finds a given topic of discussion interesting. When interaction occurs around topics which are relevant to their life experience and felt needs, particularly where these are shared with others, you have truly found a way of engaging your audience. This is why the previously discussed impact question *Identification with content?* is so foundational. However, as we will see next, social learning is not only about interesting topics and interactivity. It also matters a lot who we interact with.

3.1.4 Influence through tangible role models

According to Albert Bandura's social learning theory, "all human beings learn new behaviors primarily through observing the actions of role models – and evaluating the consequences of those actions – and then trying to emulate those actions which they perceive to be the most successful ones" (Vokes 2017). In other words, people primarily acquire attitudes and behavior from others, and any lasting change of attitude and behavior usually results from the influence of others. Interestingly, Bandura's research also showed that changes of behavior also occur when observing fictional media role models. Vokes observes that, "messages encoded into dramatic entertainment genres were much more likely to bring about the desired behavioral changes" (2017), than messages presented in a matter-of-fact kind of way. What this tells us is that if we want to inspire real change, we need to offer our audiences role models that inspire them. Films and radio drama, but also interviews with respected personalities or testimonies,   are formats which allow our audiences to draw lessons for themselves based on the observed behavior of people they strongly identify with. Role models, whether fictional or nonfictional, can be integrated directly into your content such as is the case with debates, interviews, short films or radio drama. However, getting influential people involved in the activities around your content can be equally or even more effective. Social role models have one thing in common: They shed light on the long-term outcomes of positive or negative attitudes and behavior. Due to their proximity to real life, their example or testimony is trusted by those who experience the same realities. One only needs to study the huge impact of the advertisement industry or of entertainment-education formats to realize that this is true. And if you are still unconvinced of the power of social role models, think about the latest series you have been watching or listening to and how you and other family members talk about the various characters of the series as if they were real people with whom you are beginning to establish a relationship.

The role of influencers is perhaps best observed in today's social media culture. Many of us are following at least one influencer or another, and becoming an influencer is something many aspire to. It is important to note that the influence of such influencers over others is founded on their perceived authenticity. Most of us are saturated with information and endless and often contradicting views on what matters most. As a result of this, people are increasingly looking for who to trust, not what to trust. Campbell observes:

> Facts and truth are endangered. We live in an age where science, data, and research are persistently challenged and absurdly politicized by partisan

hacks and self-proclaimed "experts". Feeling true connection online is also rare. People who do manage to create authentic connections over social media report having a largely positive experience.[14]

Julia Campbell

Because of the increasing distrust towards information, large enterprises with huge marketing budgets are also increasingly choosing to embed their advertisements in the content of strategic social media influencers. Why? Because social media influencers are able to gain the trust of their followers in a way companies can only dream of. Through ongoing social media conversations, social media influencers are able to build on the interests and preferences of followers, earning a reputation as authentic and safe role models who are worthy of trust and admiration. Ironically, research also shows that with some social media platforms, commercial algorithms greatly restrict and manipulate what information and values can be discussed. Nevertheless, influencers continue to be the first go-to place when it comes to finding not only trustful information but also purpose in life. The importance of social influencers can also be seen in nonprofit organizations. Writing about effective communication for humanitarian aid and development, Vokes states that, "Media messages should be targeted not at the entire population, but instead at opinion leaders only, who would then communicate these same messages, face-to-face, to the population at large" (2017).

We learn from the above that offering trustworthy role models to our audiences has become vital in reaching people effectively. Using role models, be it real people or fictional persona integrated into narratives, to change hearts, is not just an advertisement or fundraising trick. It is an approach we find in the Bible as well. From Old Testament prophets all the way to Jesus, the nature of God is most frequently communicated through parables and metaphors, as well as real-life accounts. The use of narratives allows us to discover God's love, promises and presence in the concrete realities of our lives. How do we do so? It is by observing the role models within the biblical narratives. We observe their attitudes and choices, identify with many of them, and learn from their lives' outcomes. Rather than asking, "What is true?", we all tend to ask, "What works?" This is particularly true, when we receive conflicting answers and information to important questions as is the case in today's media landscape. It is therefore no coincidence that most of the

---

14 Campbell 2020:loc 611–612.

content presented by social media influencers also comes in story form, presenting real-life models and narratives to follow, allowing viewers to decide for themselves who to identify with and what values to pursue.

Just as the Scriptures themselves are essentially made up of personal stories transmediated into the biblical narrative (Merz 2023), they can only really become fully accessible as they are translated back into the contemporary lives of our audiences. As we plan our activities, we must therefore ask ourselves: Do the people who are involved or presented in a given media conversation or content offer examples to follow which audiences will consider as relevant and trustworthy? Are we giving people both negative and positive role models to follow, allowing them to learn from the negative and positive outcomes of choices made by role models that are tangible to them? Do we offer different role models to different audience groups, taking into account factors such as gender, age, religious belonging, professional interests, education levels, language fluency and other social-belonging factors?

To close this section, allow me to share a brief example to highlight the power of social role modeling. During my research on participatory radio drama, we created a drama about agricultural conflict in a small village. Since there was no radio in the area, we narrowcast the drama via loudspeakers in the market and in drinking places. I was surprised by the impact. Here is just one of several impact stories I discovered during my research (2016): A local cattle owner had heard our drama in which a young herder had neglected his duty, leading to a major conflict. This cattle owner called his own herder to his house and asked him if he was getting paid enough and if everything was well, which gave the young man a chance to get more support and appreciation from his boss. The young herder was so thankful for this change in his work conditions that he called one of the drama participants to thank him, who then shared this real-life impact story with me as follows:

> Assan, over the phone on December 10, 2015: "Recently there was this guy who came to see me about…, it was a herder. He asked me whether I was among the actors who created this play, because he…, he had remembered my name. And he came to ask me and he was really very proud, because…. And he said it's something which really helped him, that he exchanged his biggest problems, him and his boss (laughs happily). He said that it (this play) really changed the attitude of his boss (the cattle owner) towards him a lot. His boss, when he heard this, he asked him 'Well, are you sure that you don't have any problems?' And when his boss asked him this, he profited to tell him about the problems he had (laughs happily). And…, really, this is what happened!"

3.1.5 Involvement

The two impact factors *Involvement* and *Independence* are strongly connected with participatory methods and the importance of investing into ownership and sustainability. However, I must add that sustainability is far from the only reason for encouraging the participation of the beneficiaries of a given ministry. This is particularly true of the factor *Involvement*. When creating ministry content and developing and implementing ministry activities, getting your audience and other key local partners involved is not just about building local capacity and ownership for the future. It is also about contextualization and relevance. Involving the beneficiaries and partners in a given ministry has the following advantages:

- Involving them guarantees that **the issues your media ministry addresses are relevant to your audience's lives**, which in turn leads to your audience identifying with your content.
- Involving them makes sure that the **solutions you offer correspond to local reality**.
- Involving them leads to **effective distribution** because participants are more than ready to spread the outcome of their work among friends and family.
- Involving them allows you to raise more **support** from your audience and partners, both moral or financial, enabling you to pursue your work with increasing resources.
- Involving them ensures you are **using the right linguistic expression** for your communication. This will increase the quality of your content in many ways: First, using the right linguistic expression increases the emotional appeal of your content as well as ensuring good understanding, as the vocabulary used will be appropriate to your topics and context. Second, local linguistic expression promotes quality conversations with your audience, giving voice to members of the community with much life experience or important perspectives, but no formal education in foreign languages. As a result, your audience will grow, attracted by the views and advice offered in your program.
- Involving them allows you to **fight social injustice**: The freedom for everyone and anyone to take part and express their views makes sure that participation truly represents the whole community as opposed to deepening already existing social gaps.

Involvement is different from independence because it is possible to pay for the involvement of representatives of a community for the purposes of efficiency, linguistic accuracy or cultural relevance, or even to create a kind of local buy-in. Similarly, it is possible to agree on the involvement of community members in a given project with the support and authority of local leaders. At times this may be the only way to start working and build momentum in a community. Other times, however, fast-tracking local involvement in this way can reduce your chances of long-term ownership. Wherever possible, involvement should not be limited to the distribution of predefined tasks among the beneficiaries or their key partners. Rather, inviting end users and partners to be involved at every stage of a project, from needs assessment to conception to implementation to maintenance, leads to heartfelt involvement and ownership. This type of involvement can lead to material or financial contribution and the contribution of know-how and human resources by stakeholders out of a true sense of ownership. To make this type of involvement possible, content creation processes and technologies, as well as the implementation of ministry activities need to be in line with the resources available to partners. This approach is very different from approaches where content creation processes, technologies, financial power, external know-how, or imposed planning procedures create dependency on outside help.

However, before being too optimistic about local ownership, we must recognize that a high level of local independence is often difficult to achieve. There are times when outside ministry agencies are only able to offer content creation or technology services, but cannot really offer capacity building. An example of this may be creating tools such as Bible apps, websites, or literacy materials for communities and partners. In such cases, beneficiaries and their partners may only be able to contribute at the development stage through predefined tasks and limited input on design questions. As a result, local stakeholders are unable to acquire the know-how and technology required to create more of the same type of content in the future. Sometimes the content created for them may turn out to be very useful to the community, but often its impact will be limited because media requires ongoing output of content to keep conversations going. This is why, where possible, we must seek to promote as much local involvement as possible, even with technologies which cannot fully be transmitted to locals. In such cases, we can, for example, emphasize the involvement of locals in the way the content is being used, to create more buy-in, and perhaps an integration of these tools into other local communication channels which are ongoing.

Despite the above, I do believe we need to be careful about our technology choices exactly because of the level of local involvement we want to see happening. Sometimes

> **Involvement should not be limited to the distribution of predefined tasks among the beneficiaries or their key partners.**

we assume too quickly, that our outside services are required because we want to see our favorite media content or technologies put to use in a given context. However, rather than assuming our content creation service or technology is needed by others who lack these resources and who often gladly accept what is freely given to them, we must ask ourselves this: Should we perhaps promote a different kind of technology or content which allows for more local involvement and ownership? For example, a number of formats such as debates, interviews, talk shows, radio drama or even music videos are especially effective when it comes to local involvement and contribution, and can be created using free software and mobile phones. Using these formats frequently not only fosters the participation of a variety of local stakeholders; it also allows them to create content for themselves on a regular basis without the need for time-consuming technical support or quality-control mechanisms from the outside. This in turn allows them to create content for using as part of the media habits of audiences, which requires a regular output of content.

3.1.6 Independence

As we've just seen, when your audience and other key partners are involved in a ministry, this can create a lot of buy-in and ownership, which can lead to long-term impact. However, involvement does not always lead to sustainability. It is possible that all of the involvement and buy-in of audiences and local partners in a program come to a halt when those initiating the program leave. This happens, for example, when the initiators keep some of the expertise for themselves, monopolize the decision-making of the program, fund most of the activities or use resources which are unavailable to the end users or their partners.

If you want a ministry to be sustainable in the long run, or perhaps even grow in momentum and width, you must intentionally build capacity in the beneficiaries and their partners in every aspect of the program. This includes building capacity in creating content but also in terms of understanding and developing media strategies. Local beneficiaries must be able to independently identify the right media formats, platforms and activities to reach their audiences as new needs arise in the

> **It is not possible to shortcut the kind of long-term momentum and collaboration across organizational and cultural barriers, which honors God and demonstrates the power of his love and fellowship in overcoming man-made boundaries.**

future. As a ministry organization, how do you make sure your local partners and beneficiaries are involved in choosing appropriate communication platforms (such as radio, TV, social media, listening groups, etc.) for reaching their (not your) audiences, rather than only giving input on such matters? How can they begin to own such decision-making processes, so that they can take solve their communication needs of the future? In terms of managing communication technologies and activities, how can you make sure your beneficiaries and partners are able to run things without you in the long run?

To counteract the inherent tendency in cross-cultural ministry for artificially pushing kingdom work through money and activism, it is vital to ask yourself: Am I investing sufficiently into building capacity in beneficiaries and their partners? This requires asking yourself another equally important question: As I build capacity in others, what am I learning from others? What are we learning together? It is only when learning goes both ways and results from solving problems together that we can truly release others towards increased ownership and self-confidence. Learning together and from each other in this way however means that activities and content creation choices need to take into account the resources, technologies and know-how available to end users. Do we make room for such resources, even if this means giving up control or letting go of our quality standards? If we want to see the involvement of partners lead to heartfelt ownership and self-motivation, their involvement and contribution cannot be limited to predefined processes, tasks and activities.

For example, when we plan activities, how to we decide on the places, buildings and staffing of a given activity? Who sets the dates, budgets and schedules? Such choices play a huge role in terms of whether a given activity is seen as owned by a ministry organization or by partners. They also affect the financial or material contributions made by different stakeholders. If we want to see ministry activities gain momentum and ownership among the beneficiaries, it is important to let go of control over the logistics and timing of ministry activities for the sake of long-term impact. It is important to remember that encouraging sustainability (that is, long-term independence from external support) is first and foremost about an inner attitude of trust and servanthood towards the wider body of Christ, towards the people he has already positioned to build his kingdom in a given context and location. This inner attitude must be nourished within all stakeholders. First and foremost, it must be nourished within those who tend to have the upper hand when it comes to financial power and what appears to some as superior know-how. However, we must be careful not to tip the balance too much in the other direction. Thinking that outside facilitators should have no influence, no say, or no long-term presence at all in a project can be just as unhelpful as expecting outside facilitation to take care of everything. Independence has at times become an idol for outside aid organizations, sometimes even to the point of attempting to fast-track an idealized level of local ownership. This can lead to a kind of pseudo independence which should perhaps rather be described as abandonment.

Every situation is different, with some contexts or communities requiring more help from the outside than others, or more time to develop local ownership. Rather than pushing for complete project ownership in every instance and as soon as possible, perhaps the goal should be defined as working towards a mutual understanding of the ministry entrusted by God to his people in a given context. In the end, the things or processes we want to see take root may only play a role for a while, with other ministry activities or approaches taking their place. Discerning the one from the other is not easy. In fact, when our work does not take root, this can be very painful. It can even lead to a crisis in our faith and calling. However, in such moments too, we will often find renewed motivation and the power to let go as we look back on how we have invested into local independence.

> **It is important to let go of control over the logistics and timing of ministry activities for the sake of long-term impact.**

As we look for ways in which our work continues, perhaps in ways we did not expect, we begin to appreciate the gifting and ministry of others which God in his wisdom called to the task long before we began to make plans for them. This reminds us that it is God who is building his kingdom! It is not possible to shortcut the kind of long-term momentum that results from collaboration across organizational and cultural barriers. It is, however, a goal well worth pursuing! In the process, God will receive the glory he deserves! The power of his love and fellowship in overcoming man-made boundaries can shine brightly, eclipsing the honors we so easily want to attribute to the work of humans and organizations.

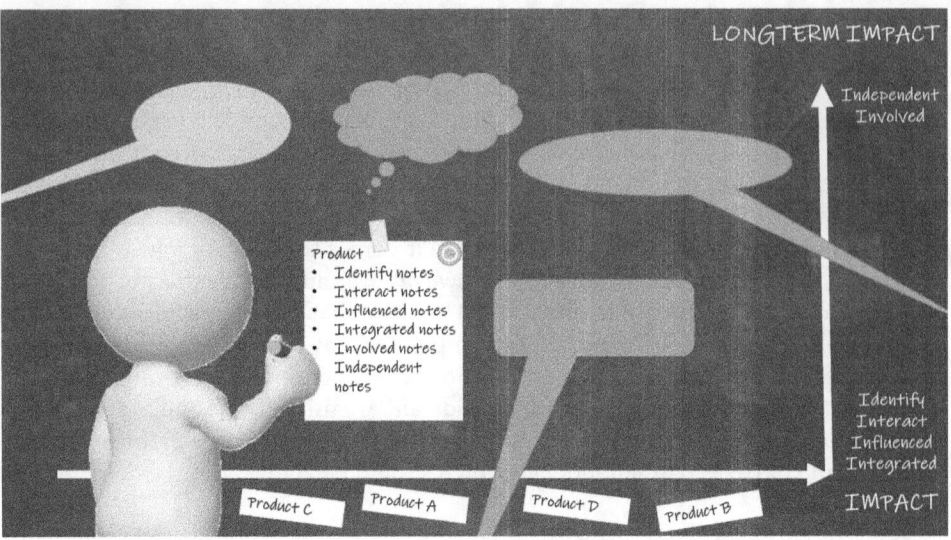

3.2 *Eyes for Impact*: A visual tool for media planning and assessment

Eyes for Impact is a visualized, participatory planning and assessment tool which is based on the six impact factors discussed in section 3.1. This tool allows facilitators and participants to discuss the six impact factors using six impact questions in order to develop effective media strategies for Scripture engagement and social change. The name of the tool finds its origin in that all six impact questions start with the letter "i", leading to a visualized plan of action. To fully understand the purpose of this tool as well as the six impact questions, let's first look at some of the challenges and barriers we frequently encounter in planning and assessing ministry activities:

- A lack of knowledge of the changing realities and needs of beneficiaries, their subgroups and their partners.
- Individuals such as managers or funding partners often have a disproportionally high level of influence over ministry activities and goals, in comparison to beneficiaries and other stakeholders, including field-based staff.
- The impact of ministry activities is not assessed. Nevertheless, we continue to fund them because of assumed outcomes and established procedures. This leads to a breakdown of good stewardship in God's kingdom.
- We emphasize the transmission of information and knowledge, versus investing into social change and dialogue. Or, to put it differently, a focus on products, technology, publication and digital content creation. As a result, we don't invest into the capacity building and partnerships needed to create contextualized media conversations.

- An emphasis on measurable outcomes and indicators. This includes criteria such as the number of verses translated, publications completed, downloads or clicks harvested via social media, the amount of content created or activities implemented. This often leads to a loss in the quality of engagement.
- A lack of input and ownership by all stakeholders during planning.
- The use of linear, closed-system planning models results in misleading expectations and reporting when it comes to short and long-term impact.
- Individual department leaders are expected to make strategic decisions and develop budgets on their own and under time pressure despite lacking the experience or information to make well informed decisions.

> "We have the habit of working by planning publications, but we don't assess the impact and information we have. We don't assess if our content or activity encourages interaction. And we don't assess if the activity or content can be used independently so that a community or group of people can take over its use. I worked with a radio station, presenting them the *Eyes for Impact* framework. They presented me with their existing radio programs, content and plans for new programs. Together, we assessed the impact level of each program and found solutions for their programs that weren't creating enough interaction."
>
> Jean-Novais Mavoungou, SIL Congo

Poor planning processes not only lead to unhelpful objectives and activities. They can also make it almost impossible to recognize, stop or amend ineffective ministry practices. This is because faulty or outdated presuppositions are not being recognized and reviewed during the planning process. This is where *Eyes for Impact* offers help. However, before describing *Eyes for Impact* more in detail, I need to point out that there are plenty of planning or assessing tools out there. Surely you will have experienced at least one or two of them. In SIL, for example, many will have encountered RBM (Results Based Management), SPAR (Strategic Planning and Review), or MAT (Multilingual Assessment Tool). You may also be aware of other resources designed to assist planners such as the SIL digital strategy guides or Wayne Dye's *Eight Conditions for Scripture Engagement* (2009). As you will see later in this book, in addition to these resources and tools, it is helpful to explore other planning frameworks developed by community development practitioners which are highly relevant in Christian ministry, in particular because of the holistic nature of our work and the need for sustainability and community ownership. All this to say that *Eyes for Impact* was

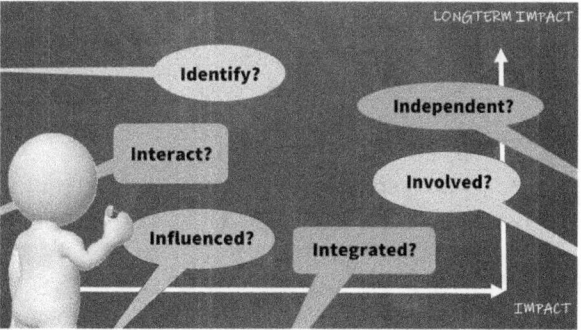

> "I learned about *Eyes for Impact* when I had just started cutting up Lumo *Mark* in the Nualu language and posting it on Facebook and YouTube one passage at a time. I realized what I was doing wasn't very interactive. In our translation team we decided to add three simple questions at the end of each clip. I also discussed our Scripture Facebook page, which promotes the translation, with two of the translators, and came up with a number of ideas for improving it. I realized I had been one of the ones doing most of the posting, but to make the page more sustainable, they came up with the idea of me leading a workshop about how to create content, which would mean they would be able to do more of the posting."
> *Rosemary Bolton, Nualu Translation Facilitator, Indonesia*

developed by taking into account other tools that are already available, while bringing a new angle to planning which addresses some of the existing challenges encountered in ministry. *Eyes for Impact* does not promise to solve all your assessment and strategic planning problems, nor is it the only way to address them. However, here are some characteristics which I consider to be unique about *Eyes for Impact* and why you may want to give it a try:

- **It is simple**: Six questions provide a clear, easy to follow structure. Rather than expecting leaders to have all the answers, the tool provides strategic questions to ask in order to make well informed decisions.
- **It focuses on the people concerned**: Beneficiaries and stakeholders are included in the process by discussing their realities and assessing their expectations and needs.
- **It is conversation-based**: Rather than allowing or expecting an individual to make all the decisions by filling in activities in a project plan, the tool allows leaders to take a step back and share the responsibility of assessing and planning with others. This process empowers those who take part and leads to a shared vision.
- **It is flexible and neutral**: Using questions allows you to avoid the bias of organizational or departmental expectations, terminologies and processes which can marginalize or even manipulate stakeholders. In other words, rather than trying to fit insights and decisions into pre-fixed categories, this tool allows you to openly explore the issues that affect your impact.

- It focuses on **behavioral and social change**, as opposed to technology or statistically measurable outcomes. As such, the tool takes into account the social factors that shape real change from within individuals and communities. This is crucial in nonprofit work.
- It allows you to **assess and plan at the same time**: Insights from assessment feed into planning, and input during planning give you the basis for what to assess next.
- It gives opportunity to **explore and learn about issues that matter, together with those to whom it matters most**. This helps prevent investing into ineffective technologies, distribution channels or activities which falsely assume impact based on oversimplified linear cause-and-effect models.

Having outlined the strengths of the *Eyes for Impact* tool, it's important to remember that its usefulness stands and falls with how well it is facilitated. This is different from other planning tools which assume a high level of prior knowledge, experience, or analytical thinking skills. The *Eyes for Impact* tool allows relatively inexperienced planners to make well informed decisions based on the experience and insights of others. Its six impact questions provide guidance throughout the process, as well as acting as a kind of safeguard, making sure the most important factors have been taking into account. However, while the *Eyes for Impact* tool does not expect a broad base of experiences or strong analytical skills, it does require good facilitation skills. As a result, decision makers may need to receive training to use the method to its full potential. This, however, is in my view an investment which has many advantages for anyone in a leadership role.

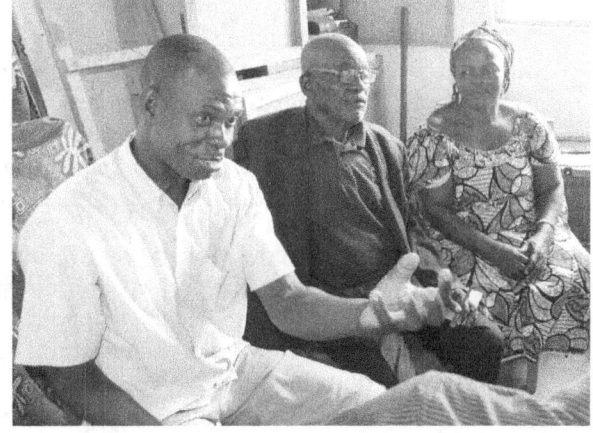

The facilitation of participatory decision-making has become very important in cross-cultural ministry. In fact, the successful facilitation of decision-making and implementation processes has perhaps become one of the most decisive skills in today's Christian ministry contexts. This is because these days a great variety of propositions and contributions by different organizations and individuals are brought to the table in any given project. This includes different ministry approaches and methods, funding models, technologies, relationships and networks, cultural knowledge, as well as differences in communication, planning and leadership styles. For most decision makers it has become impossible to have experience with, or at least understand all of the current options that come together in a program. Nevertheless, we often run entire ministry programs on this very expectation, sometimes for years. Not only do we often burden individual decision makers with too much responsibility. We also sometimes assume that all is going well, as long as we receive regular reports which confirm the predefined ministry outcomes, which were built into the project plan before budgets were approved. As a result, we continue for years with the same activities, without ever considering a change of approach which may be more effective given the limited resources God has entrusted us with.

In this context, how can we overcome the challenge of poor project planning and assessment? How can ministry leaders prioritize between different options and lead effective decision-making processes which result in realistic and well-informed plans? To address this challenge, *Eyes for Impact* helps department coordinators make use of the expertise and experience of all the staff in their departments while connecting their team with representatives of the beneficiary community and its partners. Giving voice to all stakeholders in this way builds cohesion and ownership around well-informed plans. It is also highly motivating for everyone involved.

It is easy to think that the end result of participatory planning processes should be improved practical collaboration or shared vision. While this is true, the conversational nature of the process has other important benefits: First, using a conversational approach leads to developing and fine-tuning a common language for collaboration. Second, the problems we want to address become shared problems as they are defined and understood more accurately through conversation. And finally, the process allows everyone to acquire new information and broaden their understanding and their role relative to one another through the inside knowledge and perspectives of others. These outcomes are precious goals in themselves which have great long-term value. They are also foundational to building a spiritual bond between one another as everyone finds themselves at the same level with others, under God's ultimate guidance and calling. For example, team leaders are able to appreciate their team members more through the process, as well as being able to connecting personally with some of the beneficiaries of ministry activities who they would otherwise never meet in person.

> "*Eyes for Impact* is a powerful and robust tool for evaluating how we can improve the distribution of media projects our ministry produces. It is simple to learn and to teach, yet deep and wide in its application. I recommend it to anyone who wants to be a good steward of the programs or resources God has entrusted your ministry with. We have added *Eyes for Impact* to our frontier media production trainings, and it has richly blessed our students as well. As we continue to teach and apply this training, I look forward to seeing the truths it contains challenge our assumptions and produce good fruit for God's glory."
> *Sam Hakes, Media Trainer & Cinematographer, Create International*

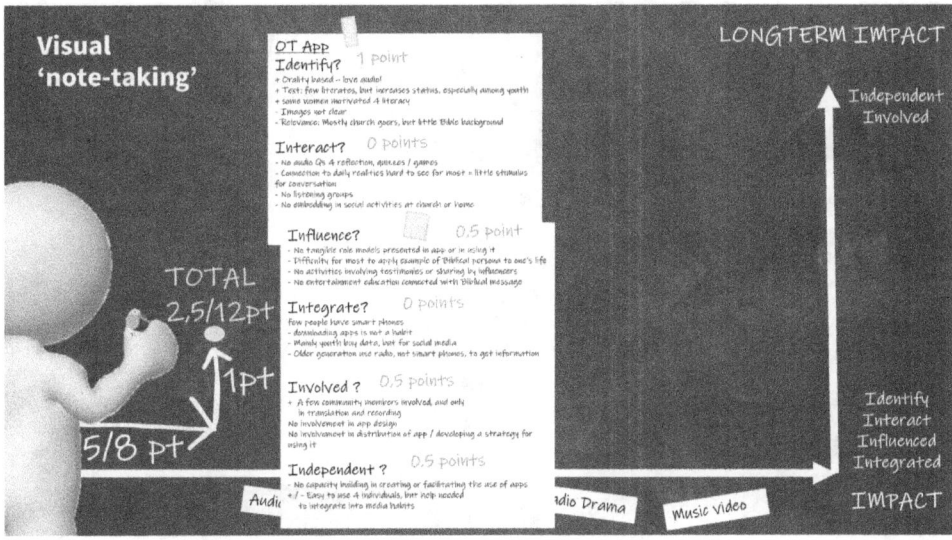

The Process: The *Eyes for Impact* assessment and planning process consists of a facilitator working with a group of participants representing all stakeholders. In discussion, the group will assess and look for ideas to improve the impact expected for existing ministry activities as well as for new approaches.

- Optional introductory step: Some groups may decide to first talk through all six impact questions with regards to a specific audience, taking notes on communication approaches which are integrated into media habits, create identification, promote interaction, influence, involve and facilitate independence. This approach will help everyone understand the six impact factors and think openly and generally about them, while also understanding their audience better. Once this discussion has been completed, the group will then move on to the following assessment and planning process:
- In the beginning of the process, the group will brainstorm the ministry activities they want to assess or consider using in their ministry. This includes publications or content ideas. All activities (publications, content ideas) are either represented on bits of paper or written down at the bottom of the *Eyes for Impact* framework. This framework may be drawn on a blackboard, on a whiteboard, in sand, on a large sheet of paper, or digitally. What is important is that all participants can see how their ideas are being visually represented.
- After a time of brainstorming to collect existing activities (publications) as well as new ideas, the facilitator will invite the group to focus on one specific activity (or publication) at a time. At this stage, the participants are invited to provide insight into positive and negative points that increase or reduce the level of impact in

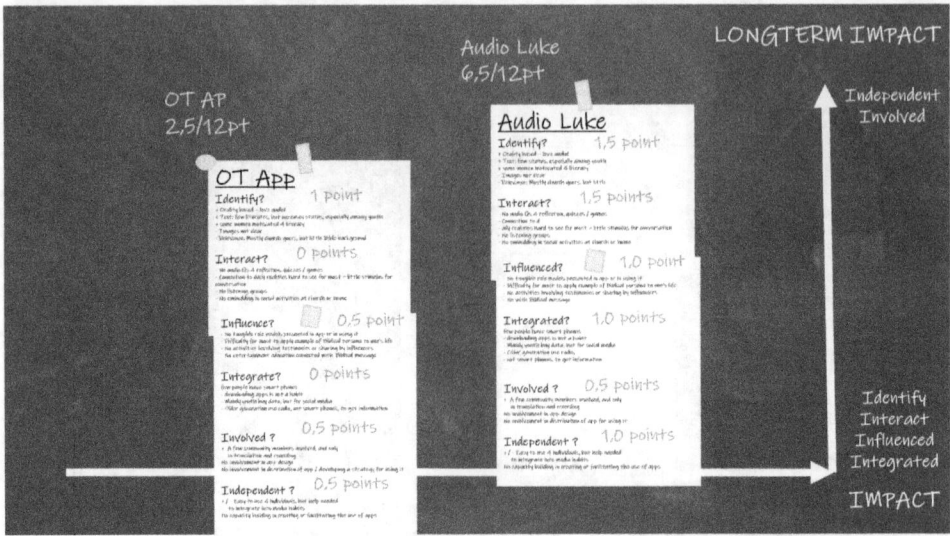

relation to each of the six impact questions, taking notes as ideas come in. Ultimately, the group is encouraged to settle on a score between 0 and 2 points for every impact question (impact factor). This process can be used to assess an existing activity (publication), or to develop new content and activities. It is repeated for every activity (publication) the group wants to assess. Where teams decide to work through several content/activities, they are not only able to see how to improve their impact for a given content/activity, but they can also compare the various ministry activities with one another and assess which ones they want to prioritize given limited resources.

Eyes for Impact session: Note taking

These are the questions the facilitator will ask for each of the six impact factors:

Identify
with content

Is the content relevant to the interests, realities, felt needs, religious attitudes and worldview of end users?
What communication and learning forms do users prefer (written, oral, audiovisual, face-to-face, abstract versus narratives, individual versus communal, etc.)?
Are illustrations, colours, graphic design and language choices appropriate and engaging for end users?

Integrated
into media habits

Does the platform/ program make use of the media habits of the audience for maximum engagement on an ongoing basis?
Is target audience using radio/TV/social media? How and when?

Interact
with others

Can the audience interact with others to express their views, suggest topics, comment or ask questions?
Does the interaction provide identity and safety by belonging to a social group?

Influenced
by tangible role models

Does the product / program provide tangible role models / influencers (negative or positive, personal face-to-face or media role models)?
Is the example of social role models embedded in authentic real-life experience (testimonies, interviews, films, radio drama, debates, documentaries, etc.)?

Involved

Are target audience and key leaders and partners involved in making choices about the program and platform?
Are they involved in creating content and in running the platform and program?

Independent

Do local resources and training of users, key leaders and partners make it possible to continue running the program / platform and create content without external help?

The six impact questions can be discussed in any order the group wants, as long as the group focuses on one activity (publication) at a time. In fact, often discussing one of the impact factors will lead to discussing and taking notes on another related impact  factor. Having said this, the most helpful order in most cases is to first deal with the two communication design questions *Integrated* and *Identification*, before moving to the social learning and inner change questions *Interactivity* and *Influence*. Once these issues are understood, it is much easier to deal with the sustainability factors *Involvement* and *Independence*. The target audience can either be defined in the beginning of the process or through the process. In any case, the *Eyes for Impact* process usually leads to a better understanding and appreciation of the subgroups of a given target community and how engaging them requires a variety of specific, tailor-made activities and content.

It is important to note that the first four impact questions (*Integrated, Identification, Interactivity, Influence*) are linked to promoting direct impact, while the last two questions (*Involvement, Independence*) relate to the long-term impact of your ministry. The reason why the long-term impact questions are situated on the vertical axis, as opposed to being on the same axis as your factors for direct impact is that promoting long-term impact often requires investing into participation and capacity building in ways that use up of some of your limited resources for promoting direct impact. Another important observation to make is that while there is great overlap between all of the six impact questions, there is a particularly strong overlap between three pairs of questions: The two questions *Identification?* and *Integrated?* are both to do with the technical design of our communication. The pair of questions *Interactivity?* and *Influence?* are both centered on social and behavioral change. And finally, the two questions *Involvement?* and *Independence?* work together in highlighting the long-term impact issues that need considering.

It is important that the facilitator gives space and freedom to the participants to make the discussion their own and speak out freely, so that the discussion becomes lively and ideas can flow freely. However, it is equally important that the facilitator leads the discussion in a way that there is agreement and clarity on what the final score should be for each impact factor and why. Clarifying what has been decided leads to a sense of safety and motivation among the participants. Generally, if the group is assessing an existing content/activity, the discussion can start with talking about how the audience identifies with the existing content. If, however, the group is aiming to develop a new media program, the group could start with identifying the audience and then discuss how to integrate the program into its media habits, before moving on to other questions.

> **The most helpful order in most cases is to deal with the two communication design questions *Integrated* and *Identification* first, before moving to the social learning and inner change questions *Interactivity* and *Influence*. Once these issues are understood, it is much easier to deal with the sustainability factors *Involvement* and *Independence*.**

> "Now I don't work anymore without *Eyes for Impact*! I first used the tool with a group of teenage mothers we have been ministering to for years. As they took part in the session, I discovered we completely missed the point with the book we produced for them and realized that they actually prefer get-togethers to debate various topics, learn from one another and receive information in the form of audiovisual content. Finally, I understood why our books were collecting dust in our cupboards."
>
> *Jacqueline Zoutene, Director of Digital Communications, Bible Society Cameroon*

Pages 48 and 49 show notes taken from an *Eyes for Impact* assessment and planning session. The first part shows the assessment of an existing product and distribution approach, while the second part shows an improved media approach as a result of discussing the *Eyes for Impact* questions.

Part 1. Example of *Eyes for Impact* assessment notes:

Chapter 3: Media Strategies for Social Change

Part 2. Example of *Eyes for Impact* planning notes:

3.2 *Eyes for Impact*: A visual tool for media planning and assessment

Below are a few more case studies of media approaches. All of these case studies are real-life examples of how audiovisual products have been embedded in a program of some sort to increase the impact of a product. Being case studies, they are neither perfect, nor are they appropriate for all contexts. They are simply meant to help you think about how the six impact factors apply to real situations. As you study these case studies, how would you score the six impact factors for each of these media initiatives? What would you change about these initiatives?

Advocacy video project to fight against financial exploitation

WHO?
- A ginger farming association in the North West region of Cameroon.

WHY?
- A few businessmen are exploiting the saturation of local ginger markets by underpaying local farmers while enriching themselves with resales in far off cities.
- This video and the participatory process of developing it created awareness among farmers of the potential of other markets outside of their region and the possibilities of improved collaboration among themselves to resist exploitation and generate more income.

HOW?
- A team of facilitators using a "video for development" approach (Lie and Mandler 2009) visited the area and, together with the input of local farmers, developed a film/documentary on the issue of exploitation of ginger farmers.
- This video was shared among local farmers to help them understand the value of ginger when sold outside of the region, as well as to present methods of collaboration to them which would empower them to resist exploitation and generate more income.
- The video was shown on national television, which raised the status of ginger farmers, while at the same time advertising their products.

Bringing language and culture and the Scriptures into focus via social media

WHO?
- Youth, urban, and international diaspora of a given linguistic community.

WHY?
- Rural youth tend to forget their mother tongue, culture and Christian faith as modern education and the search for employment draw them out of rural communities into large cities. The result is that they no longer contribute towards resolving local problems and building the future of their home communities.
- The diaspora community has great interest in staying connected with their cultural and linguistic heritage, as well as passing these on to their children. However, often their new lifestyle and social status creates barriers with makes it hard for them to contribute towards sustainable rural development. For this reason, this initiative seeks to promote a dialogue on topics of common interest to strengthen a sense of shared identity across social divides.
- When the Bible is linked to a topic of everyday life, people find it easier and more interesting to express their opinion and think about the relevance of Christian faith for their lives.

HOW?
- Create a WhatsApp (WA) group or Facebook (FB) page with members from your linguistic community which includes members based in urban and rural settings.
- Create a first post on a culturally or linguistically interesting topic such as local food. This post (text, audio or video) could, for example, contain elements such as mother-tongue vocabulary or phrases around the topic of food and cooking, as well as some video interviews or an audio vox pop* in which people talk about their favorite foods and how these are prepared.
- Make sure you ask both rural and urban community members what foods they have become used to and what it's like to shop, cook, and eat in their context. This approach will make it possible for both rural and urban community members to identify with your content and engage with it.
- To add a more spiritual element to your program, you can include some interview questions which link your topic to the Bible. You could, for example, ask your interviewees what the difference is between eating well physically and eating well spiritually or how one can make sure one's soul is fed healthy spiritual food and what the challenges are related to this. Along with your first post, launch a discussion in the group to ask its members to share their thoughts and experiences on the topic, as well as to suggest new topics. Based on the feedback and suggestions of the group members, launch new topics and discussions on a regular basis.

* Vox pop (Latin for "popular voice") is a frequently used format in which a variety of people comment on an issue. The resulting voices are cut into a sequence of short responses that show a rich variety of perspectives and is interesting to follow.

Scripture engagement via debates

WHO?
- Rural church members with low levels of formal education and a preference for oral learning, wanting to engage with God's Word on a practical level.
- Educated youths and adults who want to engage with the Bible on an intellectual (and practical) level, but are not given a chance to do so at church.

WHY?
- In certain churches, especially in rural areas, church leaders tend to teach and preach the Bible in a dogmatic way. Such church leaders have rarely experienced a more open, dialogue-oriented approach to Scripture, or they want to simplify God's Word in order to make it understandable for everyone. However, the result is that the Bible is presented as a collection of rigid rules, and God as a distant autocratic ruler. Such a worldview can block spiritual growth, as it seems to exclude the possibility of a direct relationship with God. It does not allow for the kinds of questions, doubts and moral dilemmas which human beings naturally experience as they become more Christ-like.
- Debates make it possible to intentionally oppose different views and draw out a variety of arguments. This allows participants to share their own life experiences and knowledge of the Scriptures, while also experiencing that it is acceptable to disagree and feel some level of uncertainty about important questions. This process lets them experience God not just as a source of rules and facts, but also as a dynamic and infinitely wise father who understands our preoccupations and situations better than we do.

HOW?
- By choosing debate topics that are either controversial or highly engaging because of their relevance to local life, you can make sure that both participants and audiences identify heart and soul with the conversation. Ask questions like, "Does the Bible forbid sexuality before marriage?" or "Is it okay to give medication to a sick person, while you are also praying for them?" These kinds of debatable questions cannot be answered with a simple yes or no, but they will draw out some strong and probably opposing reactions and testimonies, which can be enriching for everyone.
- Make sure your debate ends with summarizing the lessons learned from each other and encouraging more reflection, rather than creating an atmosphere of winners and losers.
- Debate facilitators will want to help their participants prepare a good selection of arguments, testimonies, counter-arguments, and Bible references to support their views.
- Make sure your debates take place in a way that church members can easily and regularly take part. This means letting people know about topics and the time and

place of the debate in advance, as well as always giving voice to audiences who are not participating officially, but simply want to be present to listen to what others have to say and have the chance to say something should they choose to do so. This will give others the courage to participate themselves in a debate.
- Invite a variety of people to participate, from church elders to women and youths. In this way, all social groups will feel welcome, and different views and topics will be addressed. This will also help everyone understand other church members better. You may also want to hold the debates in a more neutral place outside of a church building, so that people from different churches or from outside of the church feel more welcome.
- Record your debates and share them on radio or via social media, and let audiences suggest new topics and questions for the next debate.
- Make sure you hold your debates regularly and reliably, so that participation and your audience can grow.

Virtual Listening Groups

WHO?
- Faith Comes By Hearing in Nigeria among urban Christians.

WHY?
- In order to enable participants to take part in a regular Bible study, while reducing the cost of travel and the required time commitment. This is important for busy people living in cities with expensive or time consuming public transport.
- Holding a virtual Bible study enables people from rural communities as well as their urban diaspora members to connect with each other on the basis of their linguistic and ethnic identity.

HOW?
- Each week, a portion of the Bible is shared in audio and/or text form in a WhatsApp Bible study group for the members to listen to or read in preparation to the group's meeting.
- Questions for reflection are also sent to the group each time with the Bible text.
- During a scheduled weekly meeting on Wednesday nights, the group members interact on the questions via chat or voice messages, while a group facilitator draws out the biblical lessons from the text via the testimonies and experiences shared in the group.

Music videos to increase the impact of local church choirs

WHO?
- Church choirs in a rural community. Most members are women between 20 and 65 years. Some choirs also include a few men.
- Most choir members have not gone beyond primary school education, and so their grasp of national languages is limited.
- Much is expected from choirs as they are a big part of the life of the church, but they often receive little encouragement and can be taken for granted.

WHY?
- Many of the local choirs are struggling to attract the local youth, either because of cultural or linguistic differences. The younger generation prefers to sing more modern songs in English, the national language, or a language of wider communication, and on top of this, modern education means they have a different worldview than the older generation.
- Because at times they feel taken for granted, many choirs or choir members do not show up regularly enough for choir practice. This means they do not develop new songs on local issues of Christian faith.
- Producing a music video is highly motivating and unifying for a rural choir. They would love to get more attention and appreciation by creating music videos just like some of the urban choirs do, but there is no local know-how to do this, and traveling to a far-off studio is too expensive.
- Making a music video would also signal to the local youth that the choir is serious about modern trends, and this will hopefully attract more youth, which in turn could improve their church attendance and more cross-generational unity. Well prepared musical performances and music video albums also often inspire choirs to hold concerts in other regional churches, which encourages the development of new songs and can even create some revenue for the choir for other activities and taking care of local needs.

HOW?
- Starting with one choir, develop a music video for one song, to help them discover the process and result. Show this video during a church service and explain the goals of the project, as well as inviting local youth to join the choir.
- Aim to create one new music video per month or every two months, with the goal of creating an album by the end of the year or in two years. As you plan with the choir, make it clear that the album will include different types of songs in different languages, both traditional and more modern songs, as well as composing new songs on current issues.
- Include some snapshots from daily life in some of your videos, to highlight the connection between your message and the realities of daily life.
- If there are enough local internet and smart phone users, you might want to create a WhatsApp group or YouTube channel for sharing your new videos.
- With time, you may be able to extend the project to include other local choirs, especially if you are also training some local youth to help you with the technology and production.

4
Understanding Media Platforms

The fact that a new media device or platform has become available is no guarantee that many people will go on to actually use it.... People everywhere are less likely to take up entirely new media than to replace, or to "upgrade", their previously used formats.... Any development agency, national government or community group that is planning to use media to further its goals must first make a series of choices as to precisely which media platform, or which set of platforms, will be most likely to reach their target audiences.[15]

Richard Vokes

Understanding media platforms is probably even more important than understanding different audiovisual products. Media platforms are the technologies and services that carry our content to people and hopefully allow our audiences to influence our content through two-directional conversations. Understanding media platforms helps you think about your audience's media habits, which in turn helps you develop effective programs and content for connecting with your audience.

---

15 Vokes 2017.

4.1 Radio

4.1.1 Why?

Radio is one of the most effective communication platforms for ministry. Listening to it is free. All you need is a radio receiver or a phone with radio capability, and you can listen to radio even if there is no (or limited) access to electrical power. You can listen to the radio while working or traveling. This means you can reach your target audience throughout the day and can potentially have their attention for longer

periods of time than with any other platform. Running radio stations is not very expensive, which means that for many rural communities it is a sustainable communication platform. Radio is an ideal tool for giving voice to local issues and languages as even illiterate community members can easily take part. In cities, you will often find a number of radio frequencies competing with each other, but here too, you can reach many audiences with radio as people spend a lot of time listening to you while stuck in traffic or during work hours. Another huge benefit of radio is that it does not oblige listeners to make themselves known. Regardless of your religious or political identity, if you switch on your receiver, you can follow programs in private and decide for yourself if what you hear interests you. Radio frequencies can cross borders. No one can stop people from listening in private or listening together with others in order to express their own views. Sometimes people criticize radio for being too one-directional, but in reality radio programs can be designed to give audiences the chance to express their views, ask questions, or suggest new topics, even if they are nonliterate. Live shows will allow listeners to call in to make a contribution and, where the internet is available to radio audiences, they are often invited to respond to programs via social media.

4.1.2 How?

If radio seems a good ministry opportunity in your context, I recommend you first find out what radio stations already exist and visit them. Try to establish a personal relationship with the staff or director of a station before asking how much it will cost you to broadcast a program. Many stations actually struggle with creating good content, especially when it comes to using local languages and creative formats. Especially in community-based radio stations, radio staff either work as volunteers or receive very low salaries. They are often poorly trained in production. This means that, if you approach radio staff as partners with the same vision, for example, by offering them training, new doors might be opened to you for making use of the existing radio services and strengthening them. Having said this, in some cases, you will need to consider starting a new radio station to meet local needs more effectively. In this case, here are a few steps to follow:

Authorization

The first thing to check is to see if it is possible to obtain permission from the appropriate authority to create a radio station and use a radio frequency that does not have too much interference from other stations. Also make sure that you understand any limitations or opportunities for including the Christian faith in your programs. In some cases, your right to have a community-based radio station will oblige you to include prioritizing practical development-related topics as well as to cater to all local religious groups without discrimination. Ask yourself if and how you can reach your audiences effectively while respecting such regulations. Having to focus on concrete practical issues can be an opportunity for holistic ministry and make sure your programs serve everyone, while steering clear of pointless and divisive theological debates about matters of interpretation.

Researching the feasibility

FM radio transmission is limited in that the signal usually can't reach much further than the visible horizon. This is usually between 40 to 60 kilometers (25 to 37 miles), if the transmission power is sufficient. It is therefore important to see if there is a good place to position the antenna (for example, on a hill). The coverage radius of your broadcast also depends on the power of the transmitter as well as the height and orientation of your antenna. Another important factor for understanding the feasibility of a station is access to power. Is there reliable electrical power? Would it make sense to install a solar system so that people can listen to your program when the power is cut?

Costs and sustainability

Radio broadcasting equipment is mainly made up of a transmitter, an antenna and an expensive coaxial cable that connects these two elements. In addition, you will need equipment for your studio as well as field recording equipment. There are many Christian organizations that offer help with purchasing and even installing equipment for new radio stations, so the equipment costs should not be seen as your primary challenge. Rather, you need to ask yourself if the community is able to manage the station in the long run. Are they organized enough to pay for the maintenance and ongoing staffing-related needs of the station? When mobilizing funds for a station, start with the contribution of the community. The very process of starting a new project is your best chance to bring people together, create a sense of ownership, and allow the community to establish ways of contributing towards and managing the costs of the station in the long run. It is also a good idea to create a local income-generating project to maintain the station, for example, in the form of an agricultural project or by offering

printing or recording services. Some stations have an obligation to be nonprofit, so make sure your project does not create problems with the law. Using solar energy can greatly reduce the running costs of the station. However, no matter whether a station can generate funds for its own running costs or not, the aim of a community radio station is to facilitate community development, both spiritually and practically. And this is a goal worth pursuing, even in the face of financial difficulties.

Can radio communicate effectively in places where there are many local languages?

It is possible to manage a radio station in several languages, with one or two languages of wider communication being used for more general communication purposes such as news broadcasts or announcements. The important thing is to allocate specific and regular time slots to each language, so that listeners know when to expect their program of choice. Such programming can create a new sense of unity among local communities, as each language group feels valued but also connected to other language groups through shared programs.

Mission statement

Each radio station must have a mission statement. This should be a written document that defines the objectives of the station and guides the producers, directors, and the population in their choice of topics and issues that need regular coverage. For example, a radio station could declare that its aim is to address the unemployment of local youth, to support local farmers (for example, by providing information on the weather or on new agricultural techniques), to share the Word of God, to promote local traditions and languages, etc. Due to international freedom of speech agreements and guidelines with regard to community-owned media, community radio stations usually have the right to refuse to take a political stand or to advertise goods that have a negative effect on users, such as alcohol or tobacco. Such principles should also be outlined in the mission statement of a community radio.

How should you begin?

A community radio station does not necessarily have to put programs on the air twenty-four hours a day. When starting to broadcast, it is recommended to air programs only during certain hours or on certain days, allowing staff to have the necessary time to prepare new programs and get the community interested and involved. Over time, the hours of daily broadcast can be increased as more and more local volunteers are identified and trained.

Listening groups and radio clubs

Listening groups and radio clubs are essentially groups of people who get together on a regular basis to listen to and discuss radio programs on issues of interest to them. Group members take part in such groups because it allows them to express their views, share their experiences, and get input from others on issues they face in their everyday lives. In addition to listening to a station's programs, such groups may also become more active in taking part in local communication. They may, for example, recommend new topics, take on some live shows at the station, or even learn to create content such as radio drama or interviews for the station, perhaps facilitated by a radio staff member or someone else trained in the domain of audio recording and production. Creating such radio clubs is a powerful tool for increasing the impact of your station as they take into account factors such as *interactivity* and social belonging, *influential role modeling*, *involvement*, and *independence*. Here are a few examples of how radio clubs might be organized:

In churches	In a village or town setting
<ul><li>Choirs</li><li>Youth groups</li><li>Drama groups</li><li>Associations of church leaders</li></ul>	<ul><li>Associations of a particular profession</li><li>Student associations</li><li>Language committees</li><li>Other groups of interest</li></ul>

4.2 Social media

> In our hyper-connected age, we have the ability like never before to influence global conversations around social justice, inequality, poverty, climate change, and other hot button issues. When used strategically, the connection and reach afforded by social media and the potential to persuade as well as mobilize is unparalleled.[16]
>
> Julia Campbell

> I believe if Jesus were on social media today—besides having the supercool, Instagram-and-Facebook-verified handle @JC—I believe he would be calling ... us to move from social media to social ministry.[17]

> If you're too busy to engage, you're too busy to post.[18]
>
> Nona Jones

4.2.1 Why?

There are huge differences between different social media services such as Facebook, Snapchat, TikTok, YouTube, WhatsApp, X (was Twitter), or Instagram, and we will continue to see such platforms come and go, offering unique services in an attempt to cater for the specific needs of our audiences, usually for making a profit. However, what we want to focus on here is what all of these platforms have in common: They all allow people to connect with other people. This is why social media have become the most popular media platform of all time. In essence, social media are so hugely popular and influential because they satisfy not one, not two, but all major needs of our audiences. These needs also represent the six impact factors discussed earlier:

- **Interact with others and belong to a social group**: Social media allows people to find social belonging and freedom of expression in virtual groups as they connect with people with similar interests.
- **Influence and be influenced**: Social media allows you to find role models and be a role model to others.
- **Integrated into media habits**: In the busyness of life and with the availability of the internet, most media consumption has moved to our mobile phones. This is what social media capitalize on: Throughout the day you can quickly

---

16 Campbell 2020:loc 499.
17 Jones 2020:3 (loc 172).
18 Jones 2020:45 (loc 637).

send a message, chat or view a short video before you reach your destination or something else catches your attention.
- **Identify with content**: There is no better way to find the kind of content you like on the kinds of topics that interest you than joining a social media group that has a particular interest in your favorite topics.
- **Involvement**: Social media are known for being fantastic catalyzers for starting powerful movements for change, whether political in nature, ideological, or religious. The reason is this: social media allow people to be involved, to be a part of the whole process, shaping its outcome and contributing through real commitment in ideas, time, effort, and money.
- **Independence**: Social media allow users to take things into their own hands, and not depend on others. This too, is hugely attractive to our audiences and impactful.

4.2.2 How?

Considering the huge impact of social media, here are a few principles for using them effectively for Christian ministry:

- Using social media allows you to **understand and connect with specific groups of people** through existing networks. Rather than creating a social media platform right from the start that is under your control, perhaps you want to join an existing one to observe what kinds of topics are being talked about and what issues really concern your audience.
Over time this may allow you to invite group members to a new social media group where you can address some of the issues your audiences face more effectively.
- Social media is no magic solution to all communication problems. In social media too, people's attention is divided, and there are many competing networks that make real dialogue almost impossible. Often people get frustrated with the kinds of things people post or with not being able to complete a discussion because someone has suddenly posted a new thread on an entirely different topic. Social media actually demonstrates to us how little attention we often give to others. As a result, we must **be extra careful to listen well and be faithful to conversations** started by others, as opposed to using other people's comments or questions to quickly bring in our Christian message. Let the message come out of authentic questions from the audience.

- People tend to give you 10 seconds of their time to see if you have something interesting to say or if you are interested in them. We must therefore **use audiovisual formats that foster dialogue**. Short and engaging videos, images, and texts, which serve as a starting point for a discussion, are more effective than content that provides all the answers.
- **Build your audience over time**: The more your target audience knows you, likes you, and trusts you, the more regularly they will engage with your content and platform. If you want to build that kind of following, you will need to do more than post content every now and then. You will need to post content regularly on new topics and post content based on the recommendations of your audience. You will also need to respond personally to what people have to say, showing that you value their views and are also learning from them. This takes time and dedicated financial and human resources. Financial and organizational support can be difficult to obtain for such resources. If you do manage to obtain such support, investing into regular (and where possible) personal interaction with social media users is an investment that is well worth it. Building an audience can happen organically, or can be achieved through placing advertisements that use a social media's algorithms to gain the attention of specific audiences. However, be careful not to aim for artificially blowing up your reach through statistics only. Your impact depends on the quality of personal conversations you have, not on the number of followers, likes or clicks your content may generate.
- **Provide an interesting framework** for your social media, define the "house rules". This gives your audience the safety and reassurance they need to know about how to play by the rules. Here is an example: Say you have created a WhatsApp group called "Youth United" to connect urban youth from a given language community with rural youth. You start posting pictures and videos of rural and city life, while inviting members to post videos taken from their daily lives. This approach might not make the group's purpose clear enough for everyone. The group might fill up the space with all kinds of uninteresting and unrelated pictures and messages, and members might lose interest because of this. On the other hand, if you name your group "Village or town?" and you present a new question at the beginning of each week/month on a new topic, asking the members of the group to say why they prefer life in town or in the village when thinking about this topic. This framework encourages members to regularly express their views. You could, for example, ask questions such as, "What is your favorite food where you live and what do you miss?" Other topics could be things such as school, the cost of living, health care, church, transportation, etc.
- In many cases, you will want **people of influence** to handle your social media conversations. Influencers can be people who are able to lead a social media group, but they can also be influential group members. Media saturation has brought increasing distrust towards media, and an increase in audience segmentation. As a result, audiences are increasingly looking for interaction with interest groups and role models that they consider to be trustworthy and like-minded.

4.3 Podcasting

4.3.1 Why?

Podcasting is a way to share audio or video content through mobile phone apps or websites. There are many different podcasting apps available, but what they all have in common is that they allow audiences to search for content that interests them and subscribe to podcasts they enjoy. The difference from radio is that they can choose to listen to their content at a time that is convenient to them and they usually have a great selection of content to choose from. This requires access to the internet, which your target audience may not have. However, some apps will allow you to download the content to your phone for offline listening later in the day, or for sharing the content as simple audio files with others.

4.3.2 How?

In terms of using podcasting for ministry, podcasting allows us to share content with audiences on a regular basis. This can be content you have recorded and edited yourself or which you have downloaded with permission for sharing. In fact, some radio or TV stations use podcasts to share their content with those who have missed a live broadcast and want to catch up on their favorite program at a time that is convenient for them. However, in addition to sharing pre-created content, many podcasting apps also allow you to record and edit your content directly on your phone using the podcasting app. This can be particularly useful for anyone with no audio recording and editing equipment who wants to create and share content that does not require much editing, such as group discussions, debates, Bible studies, interviews, testimonies, or sermons. What's more, some podcasting apps allow you to open up live participation while the content is being created, meaning that people who have subscribed to your podcast can interact with you or even with each other while you are doing a live recording of your content. Say you are doing a series of interviews with people about the topic of how

Christians can deal with corruption in their workplace and the peer pressure or even job safety issues that come with it. Some podcasting apps will allow you to interview your guest online via your app, while also allowing your subscribers to ask your guest questions or share their own experiences. If we think back to the six impact factors, podcasts have great potential for identification with the content because users choose the podcasts they want to follow. It has great potential for interactivity and to a lesser degree for social belonging, as some live participation is possible, even if one might not know who else is listening to the podcast. Podcasting can be powerful in terms of integrating your content into the media habits of your audience as they have the flexibility to listen to the content at a time that is convenient for them. However, this is only true if your audience actually owns smart phones and uses podcasts.

4.4 Social gatherings

4.4.1 Why?

You may find it surprising to see social gatherings mentioned here as a media platform. However, we must remember what media really is and why people use it. Anything that will allow people to obtain information that interests them, interact with others, be heard, belong to a social group, and follow role models will typically become a media (communication) habit in their lives. As such, social gatherings could be considered as one of the most effective media platforms to use for Christian ministry. People gather to listen to God's Word (listening groups), to study and discuss God's Word (Bible studies), to worship and be spiritually renewed (church services), to drink, to watch sports, to drive from point A to point B, to wait for their doctor's appointment, to take a class, to buy vegetables, to mourn, to collect money, etc. All these gatherings of people are great opportunities for meaningful conversations. This is particularly true because social gatherings are more or less predictable and regular. At social gatherings, even people who do not own or know how to use a phone can take part. Social gatherings often feel safe to people because everyone is facing the same conditions or because people know each other. Yes, there are social gatherings where perfect strangers are locked into the same space and time. However, even in such circumstances, conversations can take away the stress of spending time with each other without talking to each other or of endless waiting times.

4.4.2 How?

Whatever the social gatherings may be that your audience regularly attends, if you use audiovisual content that taps into people's desire to regularly meet with others, to express themselves, follow other people's example or simply entertain themselves to make time go by faster, much spiritual learning can happen. This can happen in a spontaneous way, or as something planned that people expect. If communicated and planned well, you can use social gatherings to record interviews while others are listening in, to launch a debate with audience participation, to create a participatory radio drama, or simply to share files for entertainment.

If you are looking for a more spontaneous experience, you could, for example, ask a few church members to stay a bit longer after church to listen to a debate you and some friends have prepared and to take part actively, if they wish to. While this feels rather spontaneous to the church members, they may enjoy the experience and it may become something you plan regularly every two weeks. In this way, you will have made use of your audience's social gathering time (media habit) to build trust and to start a significant conversation. Remember, much of the impact will take place during the social gathering. You may not want to record any of the debates at an early stage, but it may well be that this time of social learning becomes popular and the participants want to share the experience with others via recordings.

Here is another example: While people are sitting in a taxi or in a waiting room, why not make use of this time by playing Christian content? This can be through loudspeakers, a TV, or even through a free wireless connection offering a selection of content for playing on mobile phones. Yes, it may be that you are not creating much interactivity (which is one of the main impact factors), however, conversations often start naturally about what is being played, and this can result in some powerful social learning. Other examples of using social gatherings for media impact include broadcasting educational content into classrooms or homes, allowing the listeners to discuss the program with each other for more impact.

One final piece of advice for connecting with people through their social gatherings. Please make sure that your ideas don't interrupt the main reason people are gathering. Make sure you "read the room" well, so that you become a welcome addition or attraction to the time of gathering, not an obstacle.

4.5 Websites

4.5.1 Why?

Websites are essentially online addresses for offering and finding information and audiovisual content. They allow you to present information to your audience, so that at any given time, they are able to find what they need. This requires that your audience knows the address of your website and is interested in its content. What draws audiences to a website is the possibility of easily finding content and information from a wide range of options, without having to store this information on their phones or laptops,

and without having to install an app. However, we must remember that most websites will not be very interactive. As such, they have less appeal to users looking for social belonging and interactivity. Some sites offer chats to users where people can engage with each other, but these chats are usually not very active, as users don't know each other. Another way websites can be given some interactivity is via links that are embedded on different pages to social media platforms such as Facebook or YouTube. This allows users to share the information on the website with others. However, because websites are mainly designed to present information and content, they are usually not very effective for keeping conversations going.

4.5.2 How?

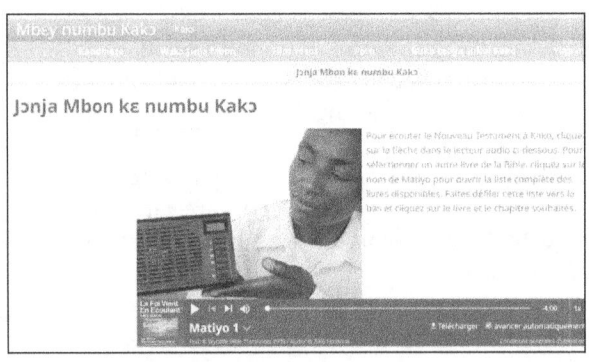

To use websites effectively, you will want to make sure you understand the kind of content and the kinds of topics your audience is interested in and offer as wide a selection of information and content as possible on these interests. You will also want to understand the technology your audience is using in terms of accessing and viewing your content: What kinds of devices are they likely to use for accessing the site? How fast might their internet connection be and how much space are they likely to have on their device for downloading files? Another major question you will need to ask yourself is how literate your audience will be and in which languages. If your audience is mostly semiliterate, consider adding visual elements to your website that help your audience navigate across different pages to find what they need. The more regularly you update the content of your website and the more your site is being shared with others through social media, the more your content will become useful. However, sharing files in itself does not create much impact. To improve impact, think about how others can download content and use it in other forms of social interaction such as sharing and discussing on social media or broadcasting it on radio or TV.

4.6 Television

4.6.1 Why?

In Christian ministry, television (TV) is mostly known for broadcasting via satellite TV. Such programs can indeed be an effective way of reaching audiences in areas with limited or no access to Christian content. In addition to satellite TV, many countries have seen a huge increase in Christian TV stations as well as in commercial or community-based stations, offering new opportunities for ministry. Of course, using TV also presents challenges. One such challenge is the relevance of content. If TV content is not created through local participation, but produced elsewhere, TV is particularly at risk of miscommunicating or being seen as irrelevant. Content created in contexts and based on worldviews and languages that your target audience is not familiar with can result in presenting the message in ways that are offensive or confusing to your audience. Images drawn from unfamiliar contexts are likely to be misinterpreted, as may be clothing styles or nonverbal communication. In the same way, testimonies to highlight faith issues may not ring true with your audience, or risk presenting values that are merely cultural, as if they were Christian values worth aspiring to.

TV is a platform that many are drawn to as it gathers members of a family or friends in front of a screen for a shared experience. While online resources such as YouTube, Netflix or video podcasts have replaced TV for many audiences, TV still offers the unique possibility of watching new content together with others without needing a fast internet connection. It allows audiences to give their minds and bodies a rest, including not having to find and choose something to watch. This relaxed atmosphere means your audience can either passively enjoy the rich and entertaining experience of moving images or enjoy discussing a TV program they are watching with others.

4.6.2 How?

If your audiences regularly watch TV, it can be very fruitful to work with their TV provider to offer content to them that uses the audiences' language(s), raises the status of their language and culture, and addresses their educational needs. Regardless of whether your audience is using satellite TV, terrestrial TV, or cable TV, the best way to work with existing TV stations is through partnership. Find out who manages the provider and try to visit the provider to get to know its staff. The more your service overlaps with the objectives of a station, be they spiritual or educational, the more opportunities you might find for collaboration through training or developing educational content in new languages that serve the holistic needs of your audience. Any content that interests your audience and demonstrates love to them, will bless them and can lead to meaningful conversations. This is particularly true for educational content. While images that are too much out of context can lead to misinterpretation, it is also true that moving images can create awareness-raising or transmit educational content, even to the point of teaching audiences new skills. Today, YouTube or TV programs such as cooking shows, DIY (do-it-yourself) programs or fitness channels have become our go-to when it comes to learning new skills. If we let ourselves be inspired by such services, our TV content can bring real help to our audiences. However, we must avoid a sensationalist approach, which tends to use the realities of this world to create feel-good entertainment, rather than educating audiences and helping them become a part of the solution.

5
Simple and Effective Audio Genres for Ministry

5.1 Different audio genres for different purposes

In the table on the following pages, you will find an overview of different audio genres that can be used for different purposes in ministry, each with its particular strengths as well as challenges that arise from using them. The list of genres presented here is not complete, but it does cover all key formats. In addition to this overview, sections 5.2 to 5.4 are dedicated to an in-depth look at audio genres, which are particularly effective when it comes to creating content through local participation, in order to make your programs more sustainable and more engaging to your audience.

Audio genre	Strengths	Challenges
Songs / Music with a Christian message can provide a memorable and powerful message that can be applied to everyday life.	<ul><li>Touch the heart.</li><li>Are easy to remember.</li><li>Song writing and music production can be a big encouragement to church choirs and empower them in their ministry.</li><li>Music easily catches the interest of all kinds of audiences, including people who are against or unfamiliar with the Christian faith.</li><li>Christian songs can be used to create music videos.</li></ul>	<ul><li>Be careful not to produce songs that have no significance for everyday life or use a "church language" that no one really understands.</li><li>Your songs should have a clear message, rather than simply stirring up emotions.</li><li>There's great competition from secular songs.</li></ul>
Sermons in local languages can be recorded during a service or in private, or broadcast live on radio.	<ul><li>Can motivate pastors in their preparation.</li><li>Builds on an already established communication form.</li><li>People can listen to sermons more than once and share them with others, including with those who aren't present in church.</li></ul>	<ul><li>Some sermons are far too long to keep audiences focused.</li><li>It can be challenging to find the balance between "virtual church" and in-person church events.</li></ul>
Stories: Well-known fictional/traditional stories or fables, as well as real life accounts can be used to communicate biblical wisdom, making it more memorable and more tangible.	<ul><li>One can make use of existing or traditional stories, as well as crafting a message from real events/testimonies.</li><li>Stories engage the heart and mind of listeners, inviting them to identify with the characters in the story and draw lessons from them for themselves.</li></ul>	<ul><li>Some stories or tales carry a negative or depressive message or are so basic (predictable), that creating a connection to the Bible can communicate the wrong message.</li><li>Not everyone knows how to tell a story in a logical and captivating way.</li></ul>

(continued)

Audio genre	Strengths	Challenges
Interviews and talk shows: Two or more people discuss a particular subject. In response to good questions, their experience, knowledge, or testimony can educate and captivate your audience.	• The listeners identify with the speakers because they shed light on the kinds of realities they themselves face in a personal way. • There is room for different points of view, which is enriching. • Allows you to present insights from experts using the kinds of questions and vocabulary your audience can identify with and understand.	• It is not always easy to find people who know how to express themselves freely in front of a microphone. • It can be hard to find good facilitators/moderators.
Debates: Two or more people debate a subject related to the Christian life. Each side tries to convince the other side of their point of view. A moderator oversees the debate, at times with audience participation.	• Very interesting to follow (entertainment-education). • Allows you to give voice to different perspectives. • The listeners identify with the speakers and get mentally and emotionally involved as they decide for themselves which side is more convincing. • Allows you to fight against legalistic or simplistic ideas about complex topics that require great situational wisdom. • Inspires continued discussion of an issue, even after the debate. • Can be used for interesting call-in shows.	• It can be a challenge to identify topics and opposing views that create interesting debates as opposed to leading to an obvious outcome. • Arguing well and building on what others have said takes some practice. • Facilitation requires experience in dealing with people so that mutual learning results from the debate as opposed to mere confrontation.

(continued)

Audio genre	Strengths	Challenges
Radio dramas are stories acted out by different voice actors, consisting entirely or mainly of dialogue. In a series, the story is ongoing, consisting of different episodes with subplots that are part of an overarching story/plot.	▪ If based on local issues and realities, audiences identify themselves strongly with the characters and events of the story, to the point of inspiring a change of attitude and behavior. ▪ In participatory radio drama, it is possible to develop and record the entire drama without a written script. This allows people, including illiterate participants, to express their experiences and views in a safe way and using their preferred language. ▪ Can be developed as a series for continued identification and impact and growing an audience.	▪ Scripting can make radio dramas seem unnatural. ▪ Participatory radio drama requires good facilitation skills. ▪ Series can be hard to develop because each episode must close its own storyline while foreshadowing and maintaining interest in the overarching storyline.
Audio Scriptures: Recordings of the whole Bible or New Testament or individual Bible books in single voice narration or multi-voice dramatization, sometimes with added sound effects and musical background.	▪ Recording the Scriptures makes use of already translated Bible texts, making them available to more speakers and useable in new ways such as apps, online Bibles, downloads, creating videos or biblical films, audio players for listening groups, etc. The unaltered Word of God can be very powerful because it puts individual verses into context. This helps prevent spiritual abuse or a shallow or even perverted understanding of God's nature and promises.	▪ Much of the Bible is hard to understand without additional explanations and interpretations.

(continued)

Audio genre	Strengths	Challenges
Radio jingles/spots: Short messages with a catchy idea and melody for repeated broadcasting.	- Can be broadcast many times per day, increasing the exposure and impact of your message. - By combining entertainment with information, these messages really grab your listeners' attention and help them connect to an idea or piece of information. - Jingles help your audience focus on their favorite program.	- When used for commercial reasons rather than for educational purposes, these can be manipulative.
Radio magazines: These programs combine a variety of formats (interviews, music, reports, quiz shows, call-in shows, documentaries) to keep listeners focused on a specific topic.	- The variety of formats keep listeners focused and curious about what will come next. - These programs are great for a thorough coverage of special events, celebrations, news, or educational topics.	- These take careful planning and a lot of time to produce.
News: Usually produced for radio broadcasting, these programs present listeners with information on recent events and issues.	- It can be a matter of safety to receive timely and correct information. - Christians can glorify God through accurate reporting, loving guidance, and inclusive dialogue in the midst of difficult situations.	- News programs can easily become one-sided or politically motivated if money or church politics influence what is talked about and how an issue is presented.

(continued)

Audio genre	Strengths	Challenges
Documentaries: A documentary is a production which offers a lot of information about a subject and gives the listeners the impression they are really where the report is being made.	• Can be used to educate people about a complex topic. • Helps research the roots and solutions of a problem by giving voice to local perspectives. • Can help bring faith into real life. • Listeners identify strongly with and are captivated by interviews with local people who are affected by an issue. This in turn makes them open to the information and advice offered by the documentary.	• The preparation (research, contacting people) as well as the production (editing together many different recordings) take a lot of time.
Comedy: Typical situations and behavior can either be imitated or described to the listeners. Comedy relies on a good knowledge of people's reactions and attitudes regarding typical daily situations.	• Very attractive (entertainment-education). • Can help to criticize behavior or values without pointing fingers. This can be helpful where negative behaviors are accepted or even protected within a cultural setting or political system.	• Risk of making fun of serious problems. • Requires a good sense of humor and a gift for observing and understanding other people.

Having looked at a few of the most important audio genres in Christian ministry, please remember this list is not complete, and there may be other formats which are worth considering. As you will have noticed, some of these audio genres may be easier to use in your ministry context than others. We will now have a deeper look at audio genres which can be contextualized more easily and are highly participative, as these are probably the most important audio genres to consider in most ministry contexts.

5.2 Interviews and talk shows

5.2.1 Why?

Interviews and talk shows are similar in that both rely on giving voice to people with unique perspectives or experiences on a topic of interest. By asking such interviewees or panelists good questions, you are able to draw out advice and testimonies that are both educational and emotionally engaging for your target audience. Whether the person you are interviewing has expert knowledge because of their academic background, their professional experience, or even due to tragic life circumstances or experiences, listening to people with real insight is highly informative and captivating. The authenticity and relevance of what is being said naturally attracts your audience's attention. This is particularly true if the interviewer or moderator knows how to ask the kinds of questions your audience would want to ask.

Another reason why interviews or talk shows are popular is that people tend to form their opinion based on observing and identifying with others (impact factor *Influence by role models*). As the interviewer and interviewees engage in a lively dialogue using good questions, your audience becomes a kind of invisible observer. As such, they are presented with the opportunity to agree or disagree with what is being said. Rather than being told what to believe or consider as important, they are allowed to think about the arguments that are being presented for themselves. In fact, even before this happens, they have the choice to consider the person they are listening to as either a positive role model, someone they can identify with, or as someone to disagree with. The choice is entirely theirs, and lessons learned in this way will last longer and be more meaningful to them than if we were to simply present them with facts and information. This leads to one final, but important, reason for using interviews and talk shows in your ministry: Neither of these genres require any significant preparation from your participants and neither require a particular educational background. As a result, finding people who are willing to take part in an interview or talk show is often very easy and a rewarding experience for everyone. Another advantage is that recording interviews or talk shows is very easy. This is a big advantage because engaging with audiences via their media habits requires creating content on a regular and ongoing basis.

5.2.2 How?

The following are some points to take into consideration, when moderating interviews or talk shows. They also apply to facilitating debates.

Ask open questions! These are questions to which it is impossible to reply with "yes" or "no". For example, instead of asking, "Do you think that all children should go to school?", you could ask "Why do some parents prefer to send their children out to the fields instead of sending them to school?"

It is often necessary to encourage participants to give further explanations as to why they take a particular stance by asking follow-up questions. For example, if someone states, "I do not think that all children should go to school. We need them to work in the field!", you could respond: "OK, that makes sense! But why not send the children to school in the morning and to the field in the afternoon?" Without follow-up questions, your interview, debate, or discussion could end up being limited to a few ordinary ideas or stances that everyone already knows, without touching on key points or interesting aspects of a particular subject. In fact, when you are dealing with participants who are nervous, unprepared, or wanting to give the "correct" answer, the lack of follow-up questions can make your production more or less irrelevant. Your guest speakers as well as your listeners will come away without having been edified, without having had a dynamic discussion, and without having been encouraged to change their minds or behavior.

If the person being interviewed is a little tense, you could try to help them to relax through questions that start a casual conversation such as, "Do you have any children?", "Where do you live?", or "How long have you been coming to this church?" If you know the person well, you can also say some good things about them: "My brother! I know that you are a really good farmer because every year your harvest is greater than mine. To be honest, that is actually why I have arranged for this opportunity to ask for your advice on field work." This kind of compliment or joking helps the interviewees relax and gain confidence. Be careful to remain patient with everyone during your interview or moderation, even when someone struggles to understand your question or goes off subject. In section 5.3 we will talk more about time management and how to handle people who intentionally monopolize the conversation. However, if an interviewee or guest does not understand a question well, this also leads to losing time and focus. In such cases, the facilitator must quickly assess if the new line of thought is worth pursuing for a while, or otherwise intervene by gently rephrasing the question. You may feel as though you are offending your interviewee or guest, but going off topic will have a negative impact on even more people as your audience will struggle to follow your program.

As a facilitator, you should try to maintain a neutral, unifying role. This sometimes means summarizing what has been said to make it more explicit or to check if you have understood what was said. You can then, without adding any comments, ask others to react to what was said. However, being neutral does not mean being unprepared or not expressing your views at all. In writing down your questions or arguments for an interview or talk show, make sure you prepare as much knowledge as you can about the subject and think about some personal experiences you have had with the topic. This preparation will allow you to enrich the conversation by expressing your insight through good questions that stimulate the conversation in a new way. Here is an example of using a question to enrich the conversation, based on your own personal experience: "The other day, a woman told me that she would like to send her children to school, especially as she regrets not having had this opportunity herself. But her husband is against the idea. Why do you think certain men are against sending their children to school?" A question like this might be used to draw attention to the fact that women are often more willing to send their children to school, while at the same time launching the conversation in a new direction.

5.3 Debates

5.3.1 Why?

Debates are an audio genre that appeals to many people. Your listeners are drawn into following along, as different arguments and emotions clash, fighting for their attention and endorsement. Naturally, your audience will try to decide for itself how much weight to attribute to each argument, based on their own life experience and knowledge. As the debate pushes everyone to side with one position or another, everyone can learn something new from what others have shared, and often people will recognize that they need to review some of their views as the debate reveals new perspectives to them. Like with talk shows and interviews, the power of identifying with others means your audience

will learn a lot from a debate. They will also own what they have learned as it grew out of their own thinking. Debates are particularly good at harnessing the natural tendency of human beings to think critically and explore ideas from all sides. Life is complex, and we all feel intrinsically that much of the pain in this world cannot be addressed by simply applying the right biblical principles. It is therefore a freeing experience for many listeners to see that our very faith allows us to grapple with theological questions as biblical truth meets reality. It is freeing to know that it can be acceptable or even necessary to oppose someone else's ideas, to argue for one biblical interpretation versus another, provided one does so with the intention of understanding the Scriptures even better. As with talk shows and interviews, debates are a fantastic genre for creating highly engaging content on a regular basis. Finding participants is often no big problem, and recording a debate is very easy. If you find ways to create new debates on topics of interest to your audience and if, in addition, you allow your audience to send in their views, testimonies, and suggestions for other topics, your content will be very popular indeed and create much fruitful Scripture engagement.

5.3.2   How?

The most important factor in preparing a debate is **finding two equally valuable positions that are debatable and connect with real life**. You could, for example, define Position 1 as "Christians are allowed to drink alcohol" and Position 2 as "Christians should not drink alcohol." In some contexts, this could already create an interesting and fruitful debate. However, if you describe the debate positions differently, this will probably lead to more depth and a more meaningful discussion. For example, someone who knows their audience well might describe Position 1 as "It is ok for women from church to sell homebrewed beer", while Position 2 is that "Women from church should not be selling home-brewed beer". Such a debate will connect the whole topic of alcohol to a local reality. It will probably draw out the same biblical teachings as our first example but, in addition, your debate will become livelier as it highlights a reality your community is facing.

Another factor that will contribute towards creating engaging and fruitful debates is your preparation. Prepare arguments and counter-arguments based on the Scriptures for each side of the debate, as well as examples and testimonies to support your biblical arguments. You can do this preparation by yourself as a facilitator, or with the participants, but your debate will become richer if the two sides of the debate do the preparation together. Knowing each other's arguments will allow them to dig deeper in the search for counter-arguments. As a result, their arguments will become more refined, and they may be able to offer more consensus to the opposing group on certain arguments. This will provide more insight into the topic as well as create an atmosphere of mutual learning.

In terms of facilitating or moderating a debate:

- Keep the list of prepared arguments in front of you during the debate. This will allow you to **highlight important arguments by way of asking a question**, should they be forgotten.
- While moderating, **gently expose errors of argumentation** which do not promote real understanding or learning: Arguments such as the Straw man, Slippery slope, Begging the claim, or Hasty generalization are ways of manipulating others or of shutting down an argument that is actually very much worth pursuing. Use questions to expose such arguments for what they are.
- As a moderator, make sure that you **create an atmosphere of relaxed but lively interaction** in which everyone feels free to speak up, even if not directly asked to do so. This will make sure no one is put on the spot, while allowing people to speak with conviction and mental preparation when they feel inspired.
- To maintain an atmosphere of lively interaction throughout your debate, you must **find ways to interrupt dominating participants**. These could be participants who take too much time to make a new point, or who go off topic. If you don't manage such people, your debate will drag out and your audience will switch off, mainly because they are confused about what you are talking about. You can manage participants who dominate the conversation in different ways, but you will need to interrupt them rather sooner than later. One way to interrupt them is to commend them on a point they have made, and ask others what they think about this point. Another approach is to state that you would love to have more time to pursue what they are talking about, but will need to go back to an earlier point made my someone.

5.4 Interactive Bible studies

5.4.1 Why?

Recorded interactive Bible studies are a powerful way of letting the Scriptures come alive. Just as with talk shows, the conversational and personal nature of a Bible study can hold your audience's attention. Your listeners will be curious to see how different people answer different questions about the biblical text they are studying. If facilitated well, your questions will not only draw out concrete ways of applying the Scriptures in daily life, but also allow your participants to talk about the challenges they face in their daily walk of faith. Showing this kind of vulnerability and being honest and concrete about difficult situations in life is very important, because this allows your listeners to identify with the participants in the Bible study and discover that God's Word speaks to anyone and in any situation. It lets them know that one does not first need to become a saint or sort out one's life to be able to study the Scriptures.

5.4.2 How?

In terms of the choice of text to use in a Bible study, you can do thematic studies in which you select a topic or a series of topics and study a few selected passages or verses around the topic. Another approach would be to simply work your way through a book and let the book raise the issues that matter to your audience through the questions you use. No matter which approach you use, continuity is important, so you can regularly broadcast your Bible study program and keep conversations going with your listeners. If you use a *lectio divina* approach to your Bible study, specific words or phrases in the text will give rise to sharing and discussion, but this usually requires participants to have good Bible knowledge and study skills. In most cases, however, you will need to prepare a few good questions to guide you through the text. Start your Bible study with a short time for greetings and small talk, followed by a brief prayer, before having one or more fluent readers read the text before you dive into your study questions. In terms of preparing your questions, here is a model to follow that has proved to be very effective:

1. Start with **3 or 4 questions of comprehension:** Your comprehension questions should avoid interpretation, but focus only on making sure the key facts and events of

the text are repeated and understood. This will give your participants confidence and help them remember the key elements of the text. First use one or two simple comprehension questions, and ask them in the order in which the answers can be found in the text. Then move on to one or two more difficult comprehension questions.
2. Now discuss **2 or 3 questions of interpretation**: Interpretation questions explore the meaning/message of the text. These should not be too general such as, "What is the meaning of this text?" or "What is the Lord telling you through this passage?" Instead, ask interpretation questions that bring specific issues to light.
3. Grapple with **1 or 2 application questions**: These questions should create a discussion on how to apply the wisdom and insights found in the text in the everyday life of your participants.

In terms of facilitating a Bible study, the same principles apply as with all other interactive audio genres: Create a relaxed but lively atmosphere and encourage people to give concrete examples and testimonies from their personal life, while avoiding the use of names or situations which may bring shame on other people. Make sure you manage the time well, and do not hesitate as a facilitator to bring your own experience and knowledge into the Bible study.

5.5 Participatory radio drama

> I have been working with a radio station in the community for a long time, but this radio station is not Christian and my objective or my intention was to have an impact through messages that will bring people to know God. There are several congregations that are involved, but we usually preach. And personally, this bothered me because it didn't allow everyone to find themselves within (identify with) the message. Now, with participatory radio drama, I have found another way to share the Word of God.[19]
>
> Abalo Kadanga

> Where development messages were encoded into dramatic entertainment genres, which invariably require their audiences to identify with some or other role model, these were much more likely to bring about the desired behavioral changes among those same audiences.[20]
>
> Richard Vokes

---

19 2023, personal communication.
20 Vokes 2017:53 (loc 1458).

5.5.1 Why?

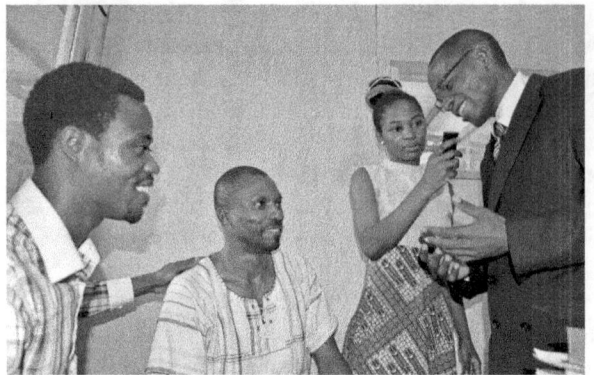

Radio dramas are stories in audio format which mainly consist of dialogue with sound effects, sometimes with added narration. Participatory radio drama refers to radio drama created with local participants based on local testimonies to address local issues. Such dramas are created using an oral story message and story development process called HEARD. Radio dramas are particularly useful for:

- Giving voice to local participants on the realities they face and in languages they prefer.
- Promoting their heartfelt involvement in developing messages and stories.
- Ensuring that the message and story as well as the characters of the drama represent local realities in an authentic way.
- Addressing delicate or taboo topics in the community.
- Attracting and maintaining the attention of listeners.
- Create cross-generational dialogue and collaboration.
- Communicating educational content in a nonthreatening way.
- Encouraging a change of behavior through audience identification with one or more characters.

5.5.2 How?

Although radio drama can also be scripted, the most effective way to develop radio drama is through audience participation. This approach relies on good facilitation of the drama development process, but it is well worth the effort as it makes it possible for any community member to take part.

Here are the five key steps in the HEARD story development process:

- Hear out heartfelt topics and testimonies
- Encourage endorsement
- Agree on needed actors and action
- Record, review and repeat improvisation until ready
- Digitally edit for diffusion and dialogue

Hear out all heartfelt topics and testimonies

Start by inviting everyone to share topics for the radio drama. It's important that you seek out topics that are heartfelt by asking for personal testimonies that give insight into why a topic was suggested. The more personal a topic is, the easier it will be for your participants to act out the radio drama at step 4.

Encourage endorsement

At this phase you want to narrow down different topics into one or two main topics. The way you do this is that the participants are asked to endorse someone else's topic if they think it is significant for them too, and everyone is encouraged to share more testimonies that highlight why this topic is important to them. The resulting testimonies will inspire your radio drama plot in step 3, and they will ensure that you choose a topic that everyone in the group can relate to.

Agree on needed actors and action

Once you have been able to narrow down the topics and issues that impact your participants, you will now want to decide with them what storyline and what characters your drama needs to highlight, both the problems but also the solutions to them. In other words, you will need both positive and negative characters to create a conflict that can carry the message of your drama. By asking who will play which role, the participants often naturally propose themselves or others. The more people in the group know their role in the play, the more active they will become in shaping the plot. Next, start by asking what happens in the first scene: What sets the conflict into motion?

Where does it happen and who is involved? Once you have developed scene 1, it will help you decide how many scenes you will need overall and what happens in the other scenes. Generally, it is recommended to complete your story in 3 to 5 scenes. Instead of developing a very detailed understanding of all scenes right from the start, start with developing the details of scene 1. For the remaining scenes, it is enough to have a rough idea of what happens. This allows you to develop your scenes progressively, and let recorded scenes inspire what happens next.

Record, review and repeat improvisation until ready

Act out and record an improvised version of scene 1. Choose an authentic setting for your recording as the background sounds will add authentic sound effects to your scene. Let your actors move freely and physically act out the scene, as this will make the dialogue much more natural. Use a single portable recorder set on low sensitivity, as this will make sure the dialogue is clear and is not overpowered by other noises. It will also make sure more than one voice can be recorded as portable recorders usually have a somewhat open angle of sensitivity and use condenser microphones, which are less sensitive to distance than dynamic microphones (see chapter 6 for more advice on recording equipment). Nevertheless, someone needs to follow the action closely and

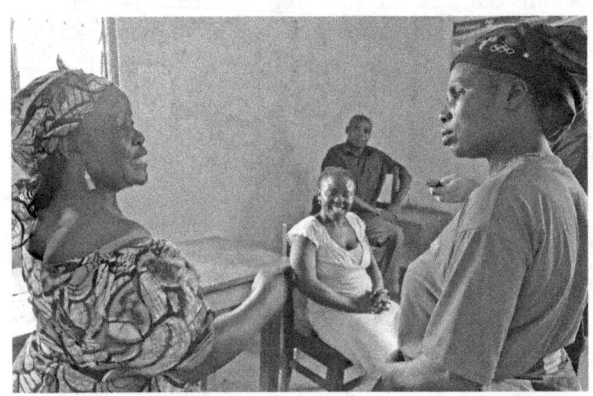

make sure the microphone faces the mouth of whoever is speaking at the moment from a close distance. I recommend keeping the microphone at between 20 to 30 centimeters (8 to 12 inches). The recordist should use earphones that are plugged into the recording device to monitor the recording level throughout the scene and catch any problems with pops caused by plosives or overpowering background noise. In order not to miss someone's voice during a change or overlap of voices, place your actors

in such a way that they are facing in the same direction. If possible, don't interrupt the recording and improvisation of a scene, even if you notice mistakes, as you want your actors to get into the flow of the scene and gain confidence. Before repeating a recording, ask for feedback, starting with positives and moving on to what can be improved. Only move on to the next scene when you have successfully recorded the previous scene in one go in such a way that everyone feels happy with it. This is usually the case after 2 to 4 takes. Before letting your participants go, come up with a title. Record your title, followed by "a radio drama created by", followed by all voice actors and participants saying their names one after another in the recording. This introductory recording will be used at the beginning of your radio drama.

Digitally edit for diffusion and dialogue

Once you have recorded your scenes and the title with the actors' names, edit your recordings in an audio-editing software, cleaning up any noises, adding some musical transitions, and adding any sound effects that weren't recorded naturally. To give you an idea of what the final edit looks like, we have included a screen shot of a completed radio drama at the end of this section, 5.5.2. I recommend using free software such as Audacity for the editing process, as this will allow you to build capacity in others who do not have the means to purchase audio-editing software. To broadcast your drama, we recommend using radio, social media, and/or social gatherings, so that your audience can respond by suggesting new topics, sharing their own experiences, and maintain conversations about the dramas they hear.[21]

When recording a drama, physically acting out roles helps to improvise authentic dialogue, as seen in this photograph of students acting out a scene in a radio drama class. Note also the position of the recordist holding the microphone.

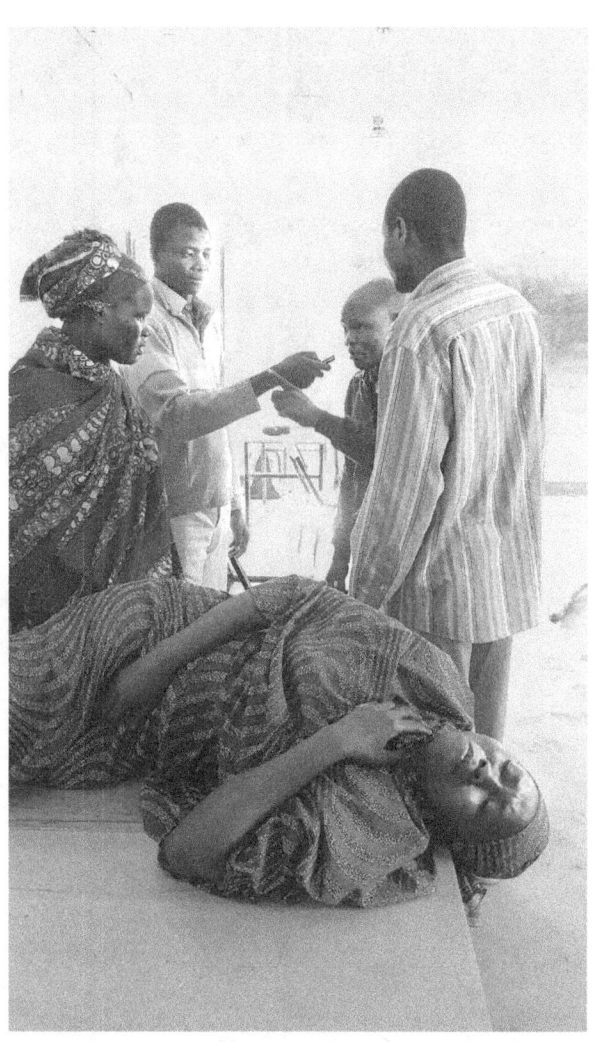

---

21 See Ernst 2021. *Participatory radio drama.*

Example of a completed radio drama

86 | Chapter 5: Simple and Effective Audio Genres for Ministry

5.5.3 Participatory entertainment-education radio drama: Communicating a message that is both authentic and transformative

The main objective of entertainment-education in general and participatory radio drama in particular is to bring about a change in the attitudes and behavior of participants and listeners. To begin with, it's good to remember that the process of participatory drama development itself already presents you and other participants with the opportunity to share God's love in the way you interact with each other. Listening to the personal testimonies and concerns of the participants helps you to develop a connection of trust with them which may give opportunities for discussing issues of faith in a personal and meaningful way. It is therefore very important not only to give voice to the realities and religious views of all participants, but also to find a way to provide hope and guidance from the Bible to them and to those listening to the dramas. When biblical hope and guidance is built into captivating stories and believable role models, God's Word, through the Holy Spirit, can become more tangible to listeners and help them overcome mental and spiritual barriers. How might this happen? Here are some principles to follow, using the acronym BUILT:

- Biblical basis, not blind boldness
- Underlying acts and attitudes
- Intentional imperfections
- Learning through long-term outcomes
- Transformation and testimony of all

- **Biblical basis, not blind boldness**: We all tend to evaluate our lives and the lives of others based on attitudes that our religious or sociocultural background has taught us, whether they are truly biblical or not. The Pharisees did it, for example, when they wanted to stone the adulterous woman. A similar misinterpretation caused the disciples to think it a good idea forbid the children to come to Jesus, and the assembly of believers in Corinth accepted sexual promiscuity among its members due to a lack of understanding. Before we integrate any message into a drama, we must therefore seek a good understanding of the overall biblical wisdom, drawing on the whole of the Bible.
- **Underlying acts and attitudes**: In our dramas, we must avoid representing Christian teachings mainly through sermons, prayers or Bible readings. In most situations, this is not authentic. Instead, the characters in our plays should act as ordinary human beings who at times fail and have doubts, while also demonstrating God's spirit in them through ordinary conversations and actions.
- **Intentional imperfections**: The characters we use to demonstrate the Christian faith should not be perfect heroes of faith. Since our listeners don't meet any perfect Christians in their surroundings, they will not be convinced by our dramas if they are full of them. On the other hand, if we show the weakness of Christians, this shows our humility, our willingness to do better ourselves, instead of just

condemning others. This approach makes it possible to question the behavior and the testimony of people who claim to be Christians, but do not live in conformity with the Christian faith.
- **Learning through long-term outcomes**: Through our dramas we must not only show which values influence (or should influence) a decision or a behavior, but also the resulting consequences. It is by evaluating the end of a story, by thinking about the consequences of decisions and attitudes seen in the life of role models that audiences find wisdom. For this purpose, we need characters who can demonstrate both good and bad behavior and attitudes. In fact, both good and bad should be found to some degree in every character.
- **Transformation and testimony of all**: Be careful not to attribute good behavior only to Christian characters. Actually, God can touch the heart of every kind of person. Sometimes, those who say they follow God don't obey him, while others who say they don't have personal faith choose to obey God. This shows that God does not show favoritism, that the Christian faith is not about belonging to a socioreligious group, but about the heart of each individual and their relationship with God.

5.6   Musical composition and song writing

> Literate and illiterate alike tell and listen to stories. Neither stupidity nor sophistication puts us outside the magnetic field of story. The only serious rival to story in terms of accessibility and attraction is song, and there are plenty of those in the Bible too.[22]
>
> *Eugene Peterson*

> Now write down this song and teach it to the Israelites and have them sing it, so that it may be a witness for me against them....And when many disasters and calamities come on them, this song will testify against them, because it will not be forgotten by their descendants.
>
> *Deuteronomy 31:19-21*

5.6.1   Why?

Music is probably the most powerful way of reaching the hearts of your audience. The combination of melody, rhythm, repetition, and lyrics means your message is packaged as an attractive and memorable experience. All of us can remember songs that were so catchy that it was hard not to sing them all day. However, considering some of the lyrics

---

[22]   Peterson 2006:loc 475.

of such songs, we often wish we could get them out of our head! How can we make use of this powerful, God-given tool for ministry?

5.6.2 How?

Christian worship songs that have been passed on as part of Church culture and translated into many languages have great value in preserving the core teachings of Christ and creating unity among believers. It is always refreshing to visit a church service far away and find the same songs and melodies that give us a sense of home even in unexpected places. However, no matter how meaningful worship music has become to Christians, it may not be the right music style for your audience, especially if it consists of people who do not attend church. Nevertheless, worship bands and choirs are often your best resource when it comes to music production for your specific audience, even if this involves song writing and using new music styles. Here are a few factors that you need to consider when recording music:

- Many church communities use a mix of old and new songs in their church services, combining melodies and instruments brought in from the outside with local melodies and instruments. Often, different music styles and the use of foreign languages stimulate different levels of enthusiasm within a congregation. In fact, preferences for either local music versus imported music, considered by some as having a higher status, will often cause conflict among different subgroups within a church. This mainly tells us how much music matters. It also means we need to understand our audience well in terms of preferred music styles and not assume that traditional music is always the best choice.
- Although music has much emotive power, we should not only promote the kind of songs that stir up emotions. As Paul says in 1 Corinthians 14:26–28, worshipping as a community must go hand in hand with understandability, having an impact on both heart and mind. I believe this to be key in understanding how to use music in ministry. While traditional and modern church songs have their place in our church services, we also need to create new and meaningful songs that speak into the challenges of being

a Christian in today's society. It is precisely by singing about current issues that secular musicians get the attention of millions of fans. Why should Christians not create music to offer alternative voices, songs that demonstrate a godly response to the realities our audiences face? If we use music in this way, our melodies and lyrics will demonstrate the relevance of the Christian faith and the very presence of God in our lives. This requires cultivating a practice of observing societal trends and writing songs in response to them. Such songs have a place both within the church and in the general community. Sadly, many churches lack such initiatives, and creating such an environment may be the best way for you to start using music for ministry.

- A good way to start creating an environment in which music can address societal issues is to organize songwriting workshops. Make sure you invite church leaders to give input on the issues that need addressing and to help craft biblically sound lyrics. This will ensure a stronger collaboration between musicians and leaders, leading to more ownership of the initiative. Another powerful way to promote music that speaks to wider audiences is by using concerts. Live events have the power to draw more attention and respect for musicians. It raises their social status and allows you to invite the community to see your musicians close-up. The musicians' charisma can draw attention to the hope that is in them, and create more interest in their recorded music. Another way of becoming relevant in society is to create music videos that visually embed your songs into the realities of your audiences.

- Developing songs for ministry requires paying attention to the language you use. You will need to find out how local and foreign languages are perceived and how each contributes to touching the hearts and minds of your audience. In addition to language preferences, you will also need to pay attention to the style of language and the use of terminology in songwriting. When composing new songs, avoid copying expressions you are familiar with from your church subculture. This kind of "church language" may feel very spiritual, but it usually carries very little meaning to others.

- Another approach is to write lyrics to address current issues from a Christian perspective and generate music for it using AI. This process works best for international languages and may not always be appropriate in terms of the available music styles, but it is certainly something to experiment with, especially for creative wordsmiths who lack the resources or know-how to produce the music themselves.

- Contrary to what most people think, producing music is not expensive and does not require a studio. Rather than buying expensive equipment or spending money on renting a studio, you can produce good quality music if you know how to use a good external sound card with two inputs, in combination with a few decent microphones and one or two portable recorders. Rather than using a studio, you can use a portable studio or record in a room with natural insulation to obtain a comparable result. Meeting your musicians in such a convenient place is not only cheaper, it is often a less stressful experience for your musicians, as they are not required to cram into a tight and unfamiliar space. See chapter 6 for more advice on equipment and recording procedures.

5.7 Radio spots

5.7.1 Why?

Radio spots are short audio messages that can be broadcast over and over again. They are usually used for advertisement purposes or for announcements. Radio spots often include some kind of dialogue or other entertaining element, which is drawn from everyday life, to grab the attention of target audiences and make the message more memorable. This entertainment-education approach, combined with much repetition, makes radio spots highly effective when it comes to planting a message in the minds of target audiences. While radio spots are typically used to sell a product, the same approach can be used to get your audience thinking about ethical or spiritual matters.

5.7.2 How?

By creating spots of real life scenarios your audience can identify with, accompanied by a short portion of Scripture, you can draw attention to the fact that the Bible is very much alive and relevant. One powerful way of getting your audience's attention through radio spots is to create a few different spots around the same topic, with the same concluding statement. As your audience hears two or more of your spots, they will want to know what your other spots might be about. This will make sure your main message is repeated many times, while the curiosity and attention of your listeners is maintained. Imagine, for example, creating a series of spots about the challenge of living in confinement during the Covid-19 pandemic, mainly to encourage Christians. You could create a series of spots about different aspects of living in confinement, one about parenting, another about fellowship when churches are closed, another about home schooling, and another about marriage in confinement or about wearing masks. If your spots are drawn from everyday experience, possibly with a touch of comedy, your audiences will strongly identify with them and pay greater attention to your message. Imagine the impact you can have on radio audiences or on social media, if each of your spots ends with an appropriate Bible verse and the closing statement, "Real freedom is in the heart!" Here's another example: Imagine creating a series of radio spots about the Bible. Each of your spots could highlight a different way in which people either misquote the Bible, misinterpret it, are ignorant of the Bible's teachings, or fall prey to others who abuse the Scriptures. Each spot starts with, "Do you have a Bible?" and ends with the closing statement, "It's not for having, it's for reading!"

Here is an example of how to put together such a radio spot:

Opening statement/ question:	Mini drama, end line:	Verse:	End statement/ question:
'Do you have a Bible?'	'God has shown me, that you will be my wife!'	'Do not treat prophecies with contempt, but test them all; hold on to what is good. 1 Thess. 5:20'	'It's not for having, it's for reading!'
Effect *for attention*	Effect *to create suspense*	Effect *transition marker*	Effect *for attention*

5.8 Audio Scriptures

5.8.1 Why?

Recording the translated Word of God is a huge need in Christian ministry. Usually, Scripture recording is done as a part of Bible translation projects. Audio Scriptures not only allow nonliterate or semiliterate community members to access God's Word, but they also make it possible to involve more people in the checking process of newly translated Scripture portions. However, church planting organizations or ministries to partic-

ular language groups often do their own Scripture recording to meet the evolving needs of the communities they serve. Audio Scriptures allow our increasingly busy audiences to listen to the Bible while at work, while stuck in traffic or working in their fields. Even literate audiences will often gain new insights by listening to audio Scriptures as the intonation and dramatization of the text brings new emphases to their attention, which they would miss when reading the text for themselves. Another huge benefit of recording the Scriptures is to fight false teachings. Similar to what happened during the Protestant Reformation, the availability and use of the Scriptures in a format and language people understand is vital for church growth and for holding spiritual leaders accountable. Audio Scriptures also help church leaders with low reading fluency or limited understanding of foreign languages to understand the Bible better. As a result, they are able to teach the Scriptures more effectively, and begin to use terminologies and key terms which they were previously unable to understand or convey accurately to others.

5.8.2 How?

Here are a few ways to produce audio Scriptures:

- **Single-voice narration:** Recording the Scriptures as one or more readers narrate the biblical text.
- **Scripture dramatization**: Different voice actors perform the direct speech of the different characters that appear in the text, while one or more narrators read the narrative parts of the story. Sound effects are added to further dramatize the text.
- **Recording Oral Bible storying**: Oral Bible storying makes sure the original meaning of a biblical text is transmitted faithfully, while attempting to minimize interpretation, but using some of the storytelling features the speakers of the language will enjoy. Recording such carefully crafted Bible stories is another way of creating audio Scriptures, including for languages where the Scriptures do not yet exist in written form.

Before recording a text, **make sure a translation consultant has checked and approved it**. The only exception to this rule may be if you want to use the recording for checking purposes, in which case it is possible to do a less time-consuming, provisional recording.

For dramatized versions, **select voice actors by these criteria**: whether or not their lives model the Christian faith, their ability to repeat phrases accurately and naturally, and their voice-acting ability. Their ability to read is less important, because a prompter will be used in most cases to speed up the process.

Use an **external sound card** plugged into your computer when recording Scriptures. This allows you to edit out repetitions or mistakes for a given sentence or paragraph and export the final version, before moving on to the next line. You will also want to use both headphones and loudspeakers, so that you and those assisting you can play back the recordings and catch any mistakes or poor sound. If you do not have a recording studio, use a temporary field studio (portable studio) built from mattresses to keep out noise from the surroundings. For more details about recording techniques and equipment, see chapter 6.

To help you manage the recording of all of your lines, you will need to **prepare a script** in which you assign a code to each line. A "line" is a sentence or paragraph that can be recorded in one go before a change of reader occurs. This will allow you to record all the lines of a person in one recording session before working with a different voice actor. It will also make finding and putting together all the recorded lines into a final edit for a chapter of a Bible book much easier. For this reason, your code should make sure that all recordings will appear in chronological order in your folder on your computer. For this to work, your code will need to start with an identifier for the book and chapter (for example, "Lk15" for Luke chapter 15), followed by a number for the chronological order (such as 001, 002, 003), followed by a code for the character (for example, "J" Jesus or "N" for narrator). An example of a script can be found at the end of this section. You can do this script preparation manually or use one of several software options that can help with the process. Another element your script will usually include is a reference text. This will show the equivalent of the line in a language you understand well, taken from an established Bible translation. Adding this information allows you to record languages you do not understand well, so that as a recordist you can keep an eye on the dramatization and make sure no lines are accidentally left out when creating the script.

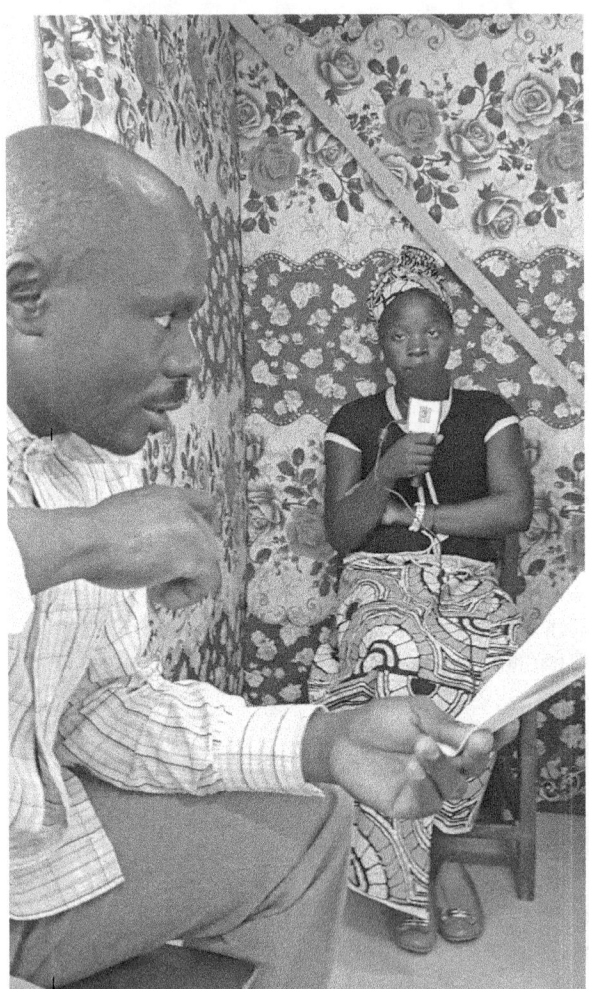

The presence of at least one or two extra readers who are also mother-tongue speakers during a recording session is highly recommended, because their presence will help catch mistakes in the recording such as forgotten lines or inappropriate voice acting. In addition, extra readers can assist the recording process by **prompting the voice actors**, that is, by modeling the voice acting so that the voice actors can focus on repeating their lines and dramatizing them well.

Following is an example of a script for dramatized Scripture recording:

Code	Text	Reference Text	Done?
L15-001N	Kanɔ kɛ kasi mɔnɔ te ɛ nya to kɛ sap sap jɔŋgwɛ kɔ Lukas 15 Ɛ Yesus lɛpɛ sendi nde:	The Parable of the Lost Son. Luke 15:11–24. Jesus continued:	
L15-002J	Wɛtɛ mbam ɓą nɛ ɓonɔ ɓembam yiɓa. Ɛ ndɛmbi te lɛpɛ nyɛ saŋgwɛ nde:	There was a man who had two sons. The younger one said to his father,	
L15-003S	"Saŋmbɛ, nyɛkɔ mi ŋgaɓiyɛ mɛyasi mɛte yembɛ."	Father, give me my share of the estate.	
L15-004J	Ɛ saŋgwɛ wan kaɓɛ mɛyasi mɛte yi nyɛ ɓą nɔ ké nyɛ ɓo. Mɔnɔ mɛtu kwaŋma kɛ kɔŋte nɛ mbɛt, ɛ ndɛmbi te dokɛ mɛyasi mɛne hɛnɛ kwą kè lɔndunate kɛ wɛtɛ mɛneti. Kumɔ mate, ɛ nyɛ si kwaŋdye kusuku nɛ kɛ nyɛm nyɛm jɔŋgwɛ. Kɛ nyɛ ma si kwaŋdye yo dete ké, yaka nɔ, nyaŋgwɛ kolɔ kɛ dyą kɛ mɛneti mɛte, ɛ yasi hɛnɛ kandɛ ɓanna nɛ. Ɛ nyɛ kwą kè diyɛ mɛsay kɛ ɓo wɛtɛ mbam mate. Ɛ mbam te kɛnjɛ nyɛ kɛ ɓakidya ɓeaɓem ɓenɛ kɛ mɔy lɔ̧. Mɔnɔ mbam kɔ gɔruma dye mɛmbumɔ mɛte yi ɓeaɓem dikima dye ké. Ko dete, mumɔ wɛtɛ nɛ wɛtɛ tì nyɛ nyɛ yaŋa na. Ndana, ɛ nyɛ kandɛ takina yasi lɛpɔ kɛ mɔy temɔ nɛ nde:	So he divided his property between them. Not long after that, the younger son got together all he had, set off for a distant country and there squandered his wealth in wild living. After he had spent everything, there was a severe famine in that whole country, and he began to be in need. So he went and hired himself out to a citizen of that country, who sent him to his fields to feed pigs. He longed to fill his stomach with the pods that the pigs were eating, but no one gave him anything. When he came to his senses, he said,	

(continued)

Code	Text	Reference Text	Done?
L15-005S	"Bɔtu ɓe mɛsay ɓe saŋmbɛ hɛnɛ nɛ ɓuɗya mɛɗye kwa, to te, mi mbɛ waka kɛ gwe nja. Mi ta tɛmɛ yɔkwɛ kɛ̀ pɛ yi saŋmbɛ. Mi ta lɛpɔ nyɛ nyɛ nde: Saŋmbɛ, mi ma kelɔ ɓeyate ɓuɗyate kɛ mbɔmbu Njambiyɛ nɛ̀ kɛ mbɔmbu wɔ. Wɛ ti yaka jeɓa se mi nde mɔnɔ wɔ na. Kelɔ nɛ mi nda yi wɛ kelɛ nɛ wɛtɛ mɔ mɛsay wɔ kɛ."	How many of my father's hired servants have food to spare, and here I am starving to death! I will set out and go back to my father and say to him: Father, I have sinned against heaven and against you. I am no longer worthy to be called your son; make me like one of your hired servants.	
L15-006J	Kɛ kɔŋte, ɛ nyɛ tɛmɛ yí yɔkwɛ kɛ̀ pɛ yi saŋgwɛ. A ɓa̧ ndi lɔndunate, ɛ saŋgwɛ ɓɛnɛ nyɛ gwe ŋgwɛtɛ wɛnɛ sɛɗye kɛ̀ wuse nyɛ kwa̧ dulɔ numbu nɛ. Ɛ mɔnɔ lɛpɛ nyɛ nyɛ nde:	So he got up and went to his father. But while he was still a long way off, his father saw him and was filled with compassion for him; he ran to his son, threw his arms around him and kissed him. The son said to him,	
L15-007S	"Saŋmbɛ, mi ma kelɔ ɓeyate ɓuɗyate kɛ mbɔmbu Njambiyɛ nɛ̀ kɛ mbɔmbu wɔ. Wɛ ti yaka jeɓa se mi nde mɔnɔ wɔ na."	Father, I have sinned against heaven and against you. I am no longer worthy to be called your son.	
L15-008J	Ko ɓekɔ ɗete, saŋgwɛ lɛpima nyɛ ɓotu ɓe mɛsay ɓɛnɛ nde:	But the father said to his servants,	
L15-009F	"Wunɛ njâki nedɔ nɛ lambo te ɛ laŋma nyɔŋɔ kwa̧ ɓɛsɔ kɔ nje lɛnje nyɛ. Wunɛ nyêki bolo kɛ ɓɔ nɛ, lɛnje sendi nyɛ mɛnakala kɛ mɛkol. Wunɛ kên ɓu̧ mɔnɔ nday te ɛ nɛ mutɔ kɔ nje wo. Wuse ɗyênaŋgwɛ, nɛ̀ wusɛ sôsaŋgwɛ, kɛto mɔnmbɛ kɔ gwa̧, ndana a womiya. A dîmbiya, ndana hɛ dolma nyɛ."	Quick! Bring the best robe and put it on him. Put a ring on his finger and sandals on his feet. Bring the fattened calf and kill it. Let's have a feast and celebrate. For this son of mine was dead and is alive again; he was lost and is found.	
L15-010J	Ɛ ɓo kandɛ jesɔ.	So they began to celebrate.	

5.9 Audio documentaries

> Suppose a brother or a sister is without clothes and daily food. If one of you says to them, "Go in peace; keep warm and well fed," but does nothing about their physical needs, what good is it? In the same way, faith by itself, if it is not accompanied by action, is dead.
>
> *James 2:15-17*

5.9.1 Why?

Documentaries are about documenting reality. As such, they are a powerful tool for awareness raising, as well as for modeling a Christian response to concrete everyday life issues. Audio documentaries are essentially made up of interviews, narration, and sound effects, as listeners are invited on a journey to experience reality for themselves in one or more locations. This makes documentaries highly attractive. By using a documentary, you can invite your listeners on a journey in which they can form their own opinion on complex issues, in the safety of observing reality from different angles. Documentaries are also effective, because your interviews provide positive role models to your audience, which they are likely to identify with and follow. Another reason why documentaries are great for creating content for people with people is that you can use your interviews and field recordings as a way of learning more about the issues you are covering, as opposed to coming into a project with your own agenda.

5.9.2 How?

In his book, *Media in Development* (2017), Richard Vokes highlights how reports and imagery from places of suffering have been successfully used in large-scale media initiatives to raise financial or political support from abroad. This is encouraging, and should inspire us to do the same, even when this is only possible on a much smaller scale. However, Vokes also warns us of some of the negative outcomes of documenting the needs of particular people groups. If the goal is to shock people from the outside into giving, this can lead to the stigmatization of people groups or even entire countries, as well as to creating more dependency on outside help. It can also lead to compassion fatigue, meaning a loss of empathy towards the suffering of others due to being continuously exposed to negative reports. Thankfully, research has led to the recognition that media initiatives can be highly effective, when they create dialogue with and among the affected people themselves, as well as connecting them directly with outsiders who can help. This is different from talking with outsiders on behalf of those who are in need. Such participatory approaches, also referred to as participatory communication or communication for development (C4D), can give voice to locals on issues of interest to them and allow them to let outsiders know how they can be of help. As you keep participatory communication in mind, below are few examples of how you might use audio documentaries in your ministry.

You can use documentaries to:

- Highlight local know-how or traditions, for educational purposes or to strengthen local identity as part of a language development effort.
- Raise awareness for and offer solutions to a socially acceptable sin or other practices that affect the wellbeing of your audience, be it spiritually or physically.
- Mobilize the support of a language community for Bible translation or language development.
- Raise awareness and mobilize prayer support for local initiatives and people that are serving marginalized people groups such as orphans, widows, or families affected by HIV. Your documentary can be created for local audiences in their language, or give voice to those who are affected to gain outside support. If the latter is the case, it may be necessary to dub your interviews into the language of your outside partners.

Planning

When planning a documentary, you should already have an audience in mind. This will influence your choice of topic and help you select the right people for sharing their experiences and views. As a next step, identify one or more locations for conducting your interviews, as well as prepare your interview questions. As you plan your location and questions, you should include at least one vox pop. This is a collection of responses from different people, "popular voices" as it were, to a set of simple questions. Your vox pop will make your documentary captivating, as your audience hears different ideas from different people, reflecting different perspectives to consider. In addition to identifying people and questions for your vox pop, think of people who can offer expert knowledge or unique experiences and perspectives to enrich your documentary. Once you have identified such people, design your interview questions in such a way that you can draw out their valuable insights. All of your interview questions should be open questions, in order to get qualitative responses. However, to make sure your vox pop questions result in an interesting mix of brief and spontaneous responses, you will want to keep them relatively simple.

Field recording

As you do field recordings, here are a few points to pay attention to:

- As you interview people, invite them to share testimonies or examples that illustrate their views, to make your documentary come alive and connect with your audience's experiences.
- Record your questions, as well as the responses, using a low sensitivity setting on your portable recorder. This will make sure background noises do not dominate your recording.
- In each location you visit, record at least two to three minutes of ambient sound using a high sensitivity setting on your recording device. This sound effect will help you recreate the ambient sound of each location during editing. As part of this process, make sure you record any greetings, small talk, or other sound effects such as opening doors, etc., that help paint a picture in your audience's mind of how you are arriving at a location and who else might be there with you.
- It can be helpful to record a narrated introduction to each of your locations while on site. This helps your audience imagine where they are and what the purpose of your visit is, especially where ambient sound effects are ambiguous.

Editing

Before you edit your recordings into a final documentary, it is a good idea to listen through them carefully and take notes of important sections. This can help you know what to use in what order, and what is not needed. It will also help you record any additional narration that might be needed. You will also want to do a separate edit of each of your vox pops so that you can cut long responses into shorter bits and make sure each question is only used once, followed by a series of short responses that are varied and interesting to follow. To achieve this, you can, for example, switch back and forth between male and female voices, or make sure shorter responses (3 to 6 seconds) are mixed in between longer responses (10 seconds or more).

The following is an example of a plan for a documentary on the impact of Covid-19 in a community:

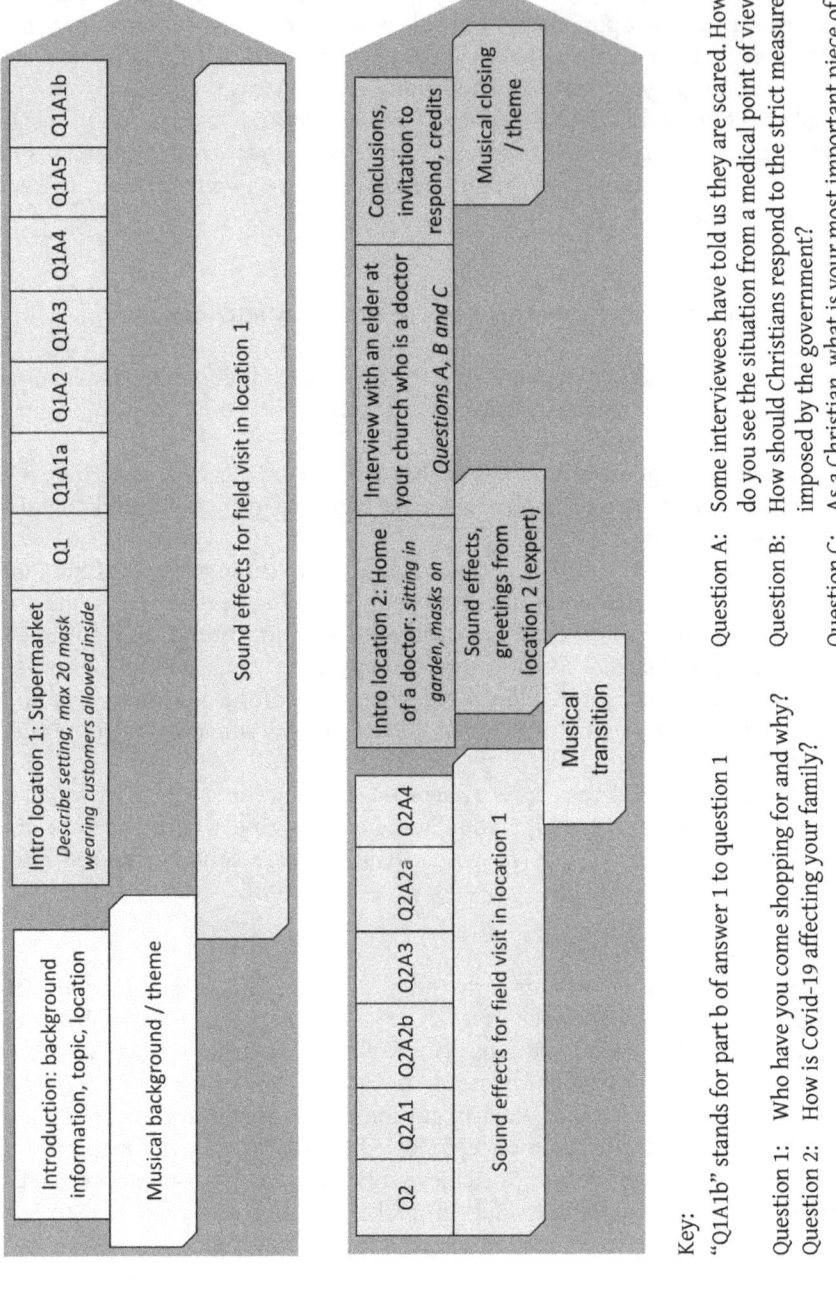

Key:
"Q1A1b" stands for part b of answer 1 to question 1

Question 1: Who have you come shopping for and why?
Question 2: How is Covid-19 affecting your family?

Question A: Some interviewees have told us they are scared. How do you see the situation from a medical point of view?
Question B: How should Christians respond to the strict measures imposed by the government?
Question C: As a Christian, what is your most important piece of advice to our listeners?

5.10 Apps

5.10.1 Why?

Apps offer the possibility of combining text with audio and images or video, all packaged in such a way that users can move back and forth through the content they are viewing on their phone. This allows you to promote literacy skills among audiences who are more comfortable with audiovisual content. The content you can offer on an app is almost endless. You can use apps to make the Bible more accessible in both text and audio format, to share visually appealing Bible stories, or to encourage Bible study and meditation through questions for reflection. Apps can even allow users to play literacy games in order to acquire more fluency in reading, to send a verse of the day to a friend, or to access a songbook or dictionary on their mobile phone. Considering the almost endless ways in which content can be packaged on an app, it is no wonder that apps appear to be media platforms in their own right. However, this is technically only true for podcasting apps, which offer continuity via sharing new content on a regular basis and creating interactivity among and with audience members. For most apps, using them effectively in ministry depends entirely on how it can or cannot become a part of our audience's media habits.

5.10.2 How?

While apps have the unique advantage of offering content in an attractive way, downloading apps is not a media habit. The big question to ask yourself is, "Will my audience use this app on a regular basis?" This also begs the question, "Does my audience currently use apps on a regular basis?" If your answer to these questions is "no", marketing your app will not make a big difference in terms of its impact. Such marketing can lead to more downloads, to more people noticing your app, but in many cases, this does not mean that your audience is engaging with the content. Remember, audiences do not tend to change their media habits just because a good product is available. What audiences are more interested in is content that they can access regularly and which regularly offers new ideas to think about or engage with. This means that regularly posting short Scripture portions in audio, text, or video format in a social media group and launching a discussion on them is more likely to create impact than simply having an app available on Google Play, which offers the entire Bible in audiovisual and text format. In other words, to make sure your app becomes useful to your audience, you will need to associate it with other media platforms and media habits that create ongoing conversations. Here are a few ways in which you can do this:

- **Create a virtual Bible study group on WhatsApp** for discussing one chapter of the Bible per day. Instead of posting the weekly passage to the group in audio, video, or text format, encourage everyone to download a Bible app for viewing the weekly Scripture portion.
- **Use your app as part of a radio program**: If your audience listens to a talk show on faith-related issues or an interactive Bible study every Monday night, for example, why not ask the facilitators of the program to read from a Bible app and encourage users to read along on their apps at home? While most audiences are more likely to simply listen to the reading, your app could include a set of questions for discussion. To encourage the regular use of the app, audiences could be asked to call in during the show and share their personal response to a question or choose a question they would like to be discussed. Your app could also include a button for sending in a free SMS to the radio station, encouraging more participation during the program.

- **Encourage the use of your app in church**: Church services are social gatherings, which by their nature fulfill most of the criteria of a media platform. If you encourage church leaders to read from a Bible or songbook app during a church service, or if they regularly invite others to do so, using the app may become one of the media habits of your audience.

6
Advice on Audio Recording Equipment

6.1 Understanding sound cards

It can be helpful to get recommendations from experienced users on different microphone models and other pieces of recording equipment. However, understanding how sound is recorded digitally will give you more confidence and flexibility in making good choices between different options that suit your budget.

Let's start by explaining the difference between analog and digital sound. When sound from a voice, musical instrument, or other source reaches a microphone through the air, the microphone transmits this sound via an analog signal or cable. Analog sound is therefore sound that is transmitted in real time as an electrical signal. However, analog sound has not yet been digitalized. For an analog signal to be recorded on a computer, it needs to pass through a sound card. This sound card converts the live analog signal into a bunch of zeros and ones so that the sound can be stored digitally. Page 104 shows illustrations of two types of sound cards which will turn an analog sound signal coming from your microphone into digitally stored sound on your computer. As you see in the illustrations, both sound cards process analog sound signals into digital signals that can be stored/recorded on a computer. However, external sound cards (also known as *audio interface*) do this before the signal reaches the computer, whereas internal sound cards process analog signals in your computer.

**Recording via an <u>external</u> sound card
(also called USB / Audio interface):**

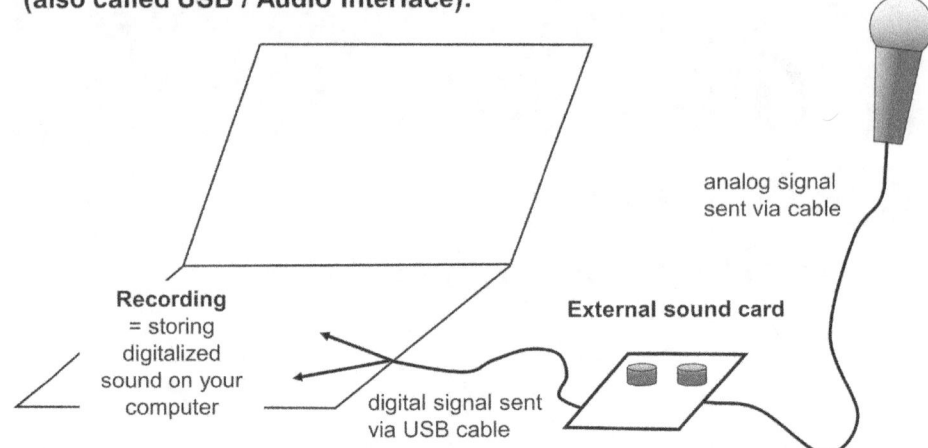

Recording via an <u>internal</u> sound card:

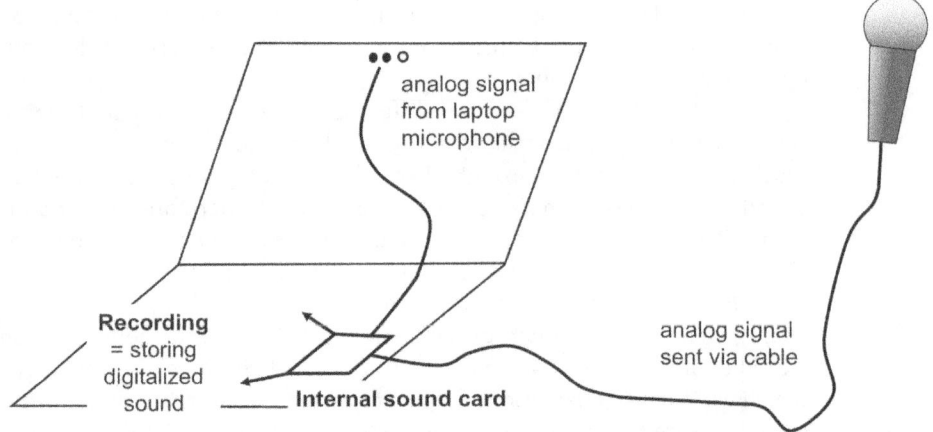

It is important to know that **external sound cards usually produce much better sound quality than internal sound cards.** This is because internal sound cards on computers are usually tiny and of poor quality as most people do not use their computers for good quality recording. Also, internal sound cards are surrounded by other computer components that emit interfering electrical signals. It is also important to note that poor internal sound cards will create a poor recording, even if the microphone you are using is excellent, simply because poor sound cards will degrade even high-resolution analog signals coming from good microphones. External sound cards, on the other hand, offer much better-quality sound processing because they are purpose-built for audio recording.

Before we look at some specific equipment, it is worth noting that internal sound cards are also found in mobile phones, camcorders, DSLR cameras, iPads, tablets, or any other electronic devices that can be used for audio recording. Again, in many cases, the sound cards on such devices produce poor-to medium-quality sound, because the processing of your analog signal into a digital recording is poor. In addition to using poor sounds cards, such devices typically use poor microphones, which further reduces your recording quality. Having said this, it is worth testing the recording quality of your mobile phone or other devices as there are exceptions.

6.2 Using sound cards for recording scripted content or music

When you connect an external sound card to your computer so you can record within an audio recording and editing software, this allows you to monitor the sound waves as they appear on your screen. For instance, this helps you monitor your recording levels. This also allows you to play back and edit your recording on the fly and save your edited recording under a specific name on your computer. For these reasons, sound cards should be your go-to equipment when it comes to recording Scriptures or other scripted texts.

Sound cards are also great for recording music. Most sound cards have at least two inputs, which means that you can record at least two different sound sources at the time. In music production this is very important because every major sound source in a musical composition needs to be recorded with a separate microphone, so that different sources such as vocals or instruments stay in rhythm, while also allowing you to treat each source separately during postproduction. Some sound cards will allow you to record every input on a different track on your computer, so that you can edit each individually for your final mix. Other card sounds will at least allow you to control the levels of each input relative to each other as you begin your recording. Another reason for using external sound cards is that they allow you to plug in good quality microphones through their XLR ports, which is often the only available connection for good quality microphones, be they handheld or mounted. XLR cables offer a further benefit: They are electrically balanced, meaning they can carry your analog sound signal over several meters, without a loss of quality. For this reason, they are great for recording in situations where microphones need to be placed at a certain distance from one another. This is a necessary precaution to make sure each microphone is only recording one distinct source, and to give voice actors or musicians some freedom to move. This is, for example, the case with Scripture recording, film dubbing or music recording.

6.2.1 Music recording principles for limited equipment

1. If at all possible, you should **aim to capture every source (instrument, vocal) of your mix separately and simultaneously**: This will ensure that your sources are following the same rhythm and make your editing easier. However, this does not necessarily mean that you need to purchase several expensive sound cards for recording larger musical ensembles. If, for example, you only have one sound card with two inputs, but your music consists of two vocals and two instruments, there are other ways to record this ensemble. You can record two of your sound sources into the sound card, and record the other two sources with portable recorders, possibly even with mobile phones. For instance, electrical instruments have outputs with clear audio signals which you can plug directly into the microphone input of your portable recording device or mobile phone, without needing any additional microphones. During the actual recording of the song, you will need to record an audible clap signal into all recording devices once you have pressed the recording button on each, so that all sources can be synchronized with one another in postproduction.
Here is a photo:

In this recording set-up, the lead vocal, who is also playing the guitar, is being recorded via a headset microphone through the first input of the sound card and monitored on the computer. The second input on the sound card is being used to record the electrical piano output. The electrical guitar signal, on the other hand, is being recorded with a small portable device (held by the seated man in the suit). And finally, another portable recording device is used to record the mini choir in the back. As you study this set-up, here are two more important pieces of advice:

- Notice that when recording electrical instruments via their output signal, the clap signal for synchronization won't be recorded. This is because electrical instruments have no microphones which are exposed to the general recording environment. That's why the piano signal is being recorded here alongside the lead vocal through the same sound card. In this way it is naturally synchronized with the microphone of the lead vocal which will also pick up the clap signal. The guitar signal, however, will not be synchronized with the clap signal. To synchronize this guitar recording with the other recordings in post-editing, you will need to boost the guitar signal in the recording of the lead vocal, because it will also pick up some of the guitar sound.
- When recording electrical instruments, you must find a way for the musician to hear their own instrument. This can sometimes be tricky, because recording the output signal of the instrument may mean cutting out the only source of listening to what they are playing. To solve this problem, use the audio output of your portable recorder to let the musicians hear the instrument, or use an adapter that splits the output signal so you can also plug in a headset (for the musician) or a loudspeaker (so that the other musicians can also hear the instrument).
- Notice also that in very rare cases, some sound sources can be recorded via the same microphone. In the photo example, above, a tambourine is being recorded together with the small choir in the back. However, before you record more than one source into a microphone, make sure you extensively test and monitor your set-up through a headset, to make sure each source is as distinct as it should be and not too dominating.

2. **It is not absolutely necessary to record in a studio**: In fact, recording in a room can allow you to place the musicians in such a way that each source can be recorded more distinctly. To avoid sound bouncing off of smooth surfaces, you can use carpets, mattresses and any other object (including human beings standing in the room), which can absorb the sound. Alternatively, you can look for a location which has rough and uneven walls or an uneven ceiling, such as mud houses with a grass roof. Also, choose a location where ambient noise is limited and avoid things like open windows, ventilators or air conditioners. To further improve sound-source isolation, make sure microphones are directed away from each other as much as

possible. In the photo example, above, for example, the guitarist and mini choir are standing with their backs towards two different walls, meaning their microphones are directed away from each other. Also, mattresses behind the choir ensure that the loud guitar sound does not bounce off the wall into the choir's microphone.

3. **Use your ears**: Every location and combination of sound sources has its unique qualities. The same is true for cables: The way your sound is transferred between different output and input signals as well as different plugs hugely affects what your signal sounds like and at what level the signal is being transmitted. For this reason, your ear is always going to be your most important assistant. Make sure every source is tested and monitored throughout your recording using a headset, and experiment with your set-up until you get the best sound possible.

Let me close this section by saying that if you cannot record all of your music sources at the same time because you have very limited equipment, you can use a method called **overdubbing**. In this approach, you can record one or two sources in a first recording, and then record the next sources while the musicians are listening to the first recording via earphones. This method requires some practice and can be quite tricky as most musicians are not used to having to stay in rhythm with a song that is incomplete. Also, listening to the other sound sources through earphones means they cannot hear themselves in the way they usually would. However, if you use a metronome, this can ensure the rhythm stays the same for each recording and is easy to follow.

6.3 Recording in dynamic situations

Medium-to-high-end portable recording devices are equipped with good internal sound cards as well as good microphones. Because they store your recordings directly on your device, they offer sound quality that is comparable to external sound cards, while allowing you to be mobile. Also, because they usually run on batteries, they allow you to do many hours of field recordings in rural environments where there is no power. Because portable recorders are light, this allows you to use them in very dynamic recording situations, to travel towards the people you are working with, or to do spontaneous recordings as opportunities arise, which in turn reduces production costs. Because of the limited space on portable recorders, they are equipped with condenser microphones, which have the advantage that they are sensitive to a wide range of frequencies. Portable recorders usually have some level of directivity, without being overly directive. Again, this makes portable recorders good for recording sound effects and music, but also for recording voices at varying distances. While mobile phones offer similar features as portable recorders, you will want to test your mobile phone to see if you can obtain the kind of recording quality you need for your projects. In many cases, portable recorders still offer higher resolution sound. For all of the reasons above, portable recorders are your go-to piece of equipment for recording:

- participatory radio drama
- debates and talk shows
- interviews
- sound effects
- an additional source in music recording

Final advice on portable recorders: While most portable recorders can be set to automatic level control, the fact that they are light and small, means you do need to monitor your recording via headphones, if this does not limit you too much in your mobility. This will help you catch noises coming from handling the device or from popping sounds caused by plosives when recording speech. Another piece of advice on portable recorders is to make sure you record vocals or instruments close to the source, using a low sensitive setting, while sound effects can be recorded from further away, using high sensitivity. And finally, make sure you only use good quality batteries and remove your batteries when not using the device, as leaking can destroy your device in a single day. This can happen if your recorder is exposed to heat or when using poor quality batteries.

6.4 Understanding microphones

When choosing a microphone, here are some factors you need to take into consideration:

1. **The direction and sensitivity angle (or directivity) of a microphone:**

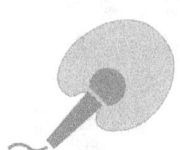

- **The unidirectional microphone:** This is the most commonly used kind of microphone. It mainly captures sound coming from one direction. It is mainly used to record vocals. These microphones are also known as *cardioid microphones* because of their heart-shaped pick-up pattern which lets you avoid other sounds such as background noises. Some unidirectional microphones are called *shotgun* or *hypercardioid microphones* because they have a particularly focused pick-up angle. They are used to record distant sounds whilst avoiding noises on the side. These can be used to record sound effects or to record a speech from a distance, or in sports. For example, this is how it is possible to hear a referee's whistle during a football match, when thousands of people are whistling all around him in the stadium.

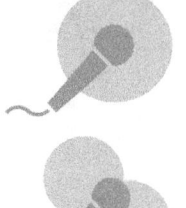

- **The omnidirectional microphone:** This type of microphone picks up sound from all around the microphone. Omnidirectional microphones are used to capture a sound atmosphere or a conversation between several people. Omnidirectional microphones are also used in lavaliere/tie microphones.
- **The bidirectional microphone:** This type of microphone picks up sound from two opposite directions. Sound coming from the sides is not recorded. Bidirectional microphones are used to record two people talking to each other in an interview, for example.

2. **The placement of a microphone:**

- **Handheld microphones:** Of all the microphones, these are the most frequently used. They are usually unidirectional and therefore made for picking up one voice, instrument or other source of sound at a time. Although they are called handheld microphones, it is good to place them on a stand for a uniform recording.

- **Fixed microphones**: Certain specialized microphones are made to be fixed in specific places.
- **Tie/lavaliere microphones**: This microphone is very small and can be attached to a shirt or tie, making it very discrete.
- **Wireless microphones**: These microphones are used to record people in dynamic situations (for example, on a stage or in a video production when the microphone has to be invisible). The sound is transmitted by radio signal or Bluetooth from the transmitter (usually connected to a handheld or lavaliere microphone) to a receiver, where it can be amplified or recorded.
- **Shotgun microphones**: These microphones are often used when recording nature sounds or producing videos. They can be placed on a tripod, camera, or on a perch above the action. Because of their capacity to pick up sound from a precise direction and a focused angle, they allow great mobility and discretion.
- **Clip-on microphones**: The microphones are great for recording sources in dynamic situations. They can, for example, be used to record your voice actors when dramatizing the Scriptures or doing a film dubbing, or for recording an instrument.

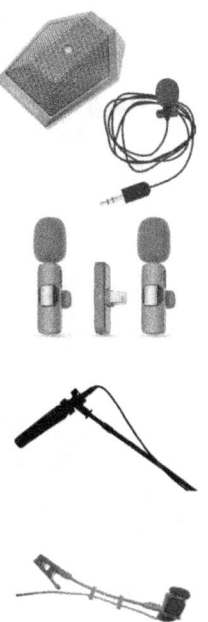

3. **The technology of a microphone**:

Different kinds of technologies are used to build microphones, and each technology will affect the power source of your microphone, its sensitivity to different frequencies as well as its fragility. The most common microphone technologies are dynamic microphones and condenser microphones. Dynamic microphones do not need any power supply. They are not as sensitive to the full range of the frequencies that are present in a sound when compared to condenser microphones, but more sensitive to how close they are placed to a sound source. This means they will not pick up certain background noises as easily, which can help with recording vocals in certain situations. Condenser microphones, on the other hand, need a power supply. They are suitable for recording a wide range of sound frequencies to obtain high resolution recordings of sound effects, vocals, or music.

6.5 Additional recording equipment

- **Stands**: These help to position and stabilize the microphone (or the camera) to obtain a balanced recording and avoid noises that result from handling your equipment.
- **Pop/noise filters**: These are used to eliminate noises such as the wind or plosives in human speech. You can make your own noise filters from a piece of sponge.

- **Headsets/earphones:**  These help you monitor the quality of your recording. It is recommended to use a good set both during recordings as well as when editing so that faults in a recording can be identified and corrected at any given time in the process. Please be aware that the balance of different frequencies in a mix (for example, between vocals and instruments or ambient sounds and dialogue) can sound very different if you play your final version on a set of speakers. If your content is intended for listening to via speakers, you may need to create a separate version of your audio.
- **Studios/portable studios:** Many recording projects are best recorded in a silent environment, which is soundproof towards the outside and where sounds from the inside are absorbed by the surrounding walls. If you do not have access to a studio,  start by looking for a room or building which offers natural soundproofing, such as rounded mud huts with a straw roof. However, more often than not you will need to transform a less than ideal room into a studio or build a portable studio in a room. If you cover the wall with egg boxes or mattresses, and the floor with soft carpets, you can prevent sound from reverberating within the room. In addition, curtains, furniture, and any other soft household items can help you cover smooth hard surfaces to reduce reverb within a room. If you only need a small space for your recording (for example, when recording Scriptures) you can set up a small soundproof recording booth, also called a portable studio. To do this, place two to three mattresses in the corner of a room between some pieces of furniture, with a single opening facing a microphone stand. This way only voices coming from within the booth can reach the microphone, while most other sounds are absorbed by the mattresses.

For advice on audio equipment in the context of video recording, see chapter 8 on video recording equipment.

6.6 Recording sound effects

As seen above, stimulating the imagination of your audience will let your content come alive in their minds. One of the best ways of doing this is to make sure your content includes sound effects. These can be specific sounds such as a rooster call, a passing motorbike, a bird, a rusty old door, the roar of a lion or leopard, footsteps on sandy ground, or ambient sound effects such as the sound of walking through a field and hearing different birds or the sound of a busy street, market, or airport.

You can **record your own sound effects** to make sure you get the sound quality you need and to make sure your sound effect is understood by your audience. This is particularly true for sounds that can be ambiguous depending on the background and experience of your audience. To take a simple example, if you want to tell the story of someone leaving by train, using a sound effect recorded at a station in Europe or the sound of a high-speed train passing by may not make much sense to your audience.

For some sound effects, it can be almost impossible to do your own recording. To record sounds like animal cries, thunder, and lightning or even a crying child, you would need to be ready at the right time in the right place. For this reason, it can be useful to carry a small recording device on you or use your mobile phone to collect different sounds as the occasion presents itself, and start your own collection of sound effects. However, when recording a sound effect is not an option, you can **download almost any sound effect from the internet**. There are many sites that offer a wide range of free sound effects, if you know where to look and as long as you test to make sure your audience recognizes the effect for what it is.

Another way of obtaining sound effects is by producing them artificially. You can, for example, create the sound of rain by rubbing a plastic bag close to the microphone. Artificially produced sound effects often don't sound natural, so this should only be done if you have no other solution. However, **creating ambient sound effects artificially can be very effective**. To create a village atmosphere, you can, for example, combine the sound of birds, children playing, and an old motorbike driving by with the sound of a dog barking and goats bleating. When creating such ambient sounds artificially, be careful not to exaggerate in terms of the number individual sounds or the number of repetitions, otherwise the effect will quickly feel artificial.

7
Simple and Effective Video Genres for Ministry

7.1 Different videos for different purposes

There is quite a bit of overlap between video and audio genres. Debates, for example, or documentaries, exist both in audio and video format, and radio dramas resemble short films. Choosing between an audio and video genre for reaching your target audience most effectively will depend on a number of factors such as the media platform your audience tends to use, the speed of internet connections, the kind of device and screen size on which your audience is likely to access your content, and whether or not your audience is doing something else while viewing or listening to your content. Generally, video genres that don't rely much on nonverbal communication are less likely to have much of an advantage over their audio equivalent. For example, listening to a debate with others or while going to work might be more practical than trying to keep your eyes on a small screen to catch the odd nonverbal clue here and there. However, don't underestimate the power of moving images! Music videos, for example, have an appeal that music in audio format does not. Below is an overview of different video genres that are useful in Christian ministry, while sections 7.2 to 7.5 are dedicated to an in-depth look at genres that are particularly effective when it comes to creating media for people with people.

Video genre	Strengths	Challenges
Music videos: Music videos are very popular because they are short, easy to share with others, and because of the frequently changing camera angles which captivate your audience's attention.	<ul><li>They have a strong emotional impact.</li><li>The message is easy to remember because it is wrapped up in repetition, rhythm, and melody.</li><li>Musicians and choirs from churches are usually very motivated when given the opportunity to perform their music to reach a wider audience.</li></ul>	<ul><li>Be careful not to imitate music videos available on the market that show a life of luxury and comfort. Such videos idolize materialism instead of promoting hope.</li></ul>
Videos based on still images: Instead of filming real situations or events, you can produce videos by animating still images (illustrations, drawings, photos).	<ul><li>They do not require video recording equipment.</li><li>It is easy to take pictures with a digital camera or mobile phone or download images from the internet.</li><li>You can create Bible-story videos using free illustrations that are available online.</li><li>You can create videos on events that already took place, provided someone took a few pictures.</li><li>Images can often highlight interesting perspectives, historic or scientific facts or emotions that are impossible to capture with a video recording.</li></ul>	<ul><li>For some types of local stories, it can be difficult to find illustrations. *On the positive side, this may be an opportunity for local artists.*</li></ul>
Animations: 2D or 3D animations have great appeal because they exaggerate the emotions and action in a story, as well as bringing people, places, and events to life in highly creative ways.	<ul><li>They can illustrate complex processes, which are otherwise hard to film or imagine.</li><li>They can be used to simplify or emphasize important elements or perspectives.</li><li>They allow you to create persona, which are stereotypical or non-discriminating and neutral, which can also make your content usable for a wider audience.</li><li>They appeal to children and adults alike.</li><li>They can be used for translating films or the Bible into sign languages.</li></ul>	<ul><li>Creating animations is very time consuming.</li><li>Some illustrations or angles in animations can be quite abstract, making it difficult for some audiences to interpret them correctly.</li></ul>

(continued)

Video genre	Strengths	Challenges
Interviews, debates, and talk shows: Guided by a moderator, one or more participants present their opinions, arguments, or knowledge in order to give viewers a variety of personal perspectives. Sometimes an audience is present that can give additional input or ask questions.	- It is interesting to follow because of the variety of perspectives as well as the nonverbal cues that occur naturally. - The viewers naturally begin to sympathize with one person or another as they identify with the person's experience or viewpoint. - Can be recorded during a virtual online meeting, if you do not have the time or equipment for recording and editing a more advanced video. - You do not need to train your participants nor do they need to spend much time rehearsing or repeating their contribution. In fact, speaking off the cuff and being relaxed often leads to the most honest and enriching conversations. - They often lead to ongoing conversations among or with your audiences, which increases your impact.	- Not everyone finds it easy to express themselves freely and behave naturally in front of a camera.
Films/short films: The story can be fictional or based on real events. Usually, one or more protagonists face a particular challenge (main conflict), but one or more antagonists get in the way. As the main plot and subplots unfold and get resolved, various lessons can be learned together with the main characters.	- Films keep the audience's attention right to the end because everyone wants to know if and how the main characters succeed in overcoming the challenges they face. - Films can present life as it is, with all its difficulties, surprises, and personal conflicts. Audiences often closely identify with the actors, making them open to the film's moral lessons. - It is surprising how little training your actors need, if you let them play a role they strongly identify with and improvise their dialogue as opposed to memorizing their lines.	- It can be difficult to develop an interesting plot. - If the film is developed using the HEARD method, this requires good facilitation. - There is a lot of competition from excellent secular films that have better actors and more impressive visual effects.

(continued)

Video genre	Strengths	Challenges
Series/soap operas: More or less based on the same set of main characters, each episode is like a short story within a larger story, which maintains the interest of viewers.	▪ Series are hugely popular because viewers identify more and more with the characters as the stories unfold. This allows you to teach your audience different moral lessons as your characters learn from their mistakes over time. Rather than having to let this happen in a single plot, this can take place over time, which is more authentic. ▪ Series create a lot of interaction with and between audiences because viewers naturally want to discuss how they view the positive and negative role models of the series and what they hope will happen. This increases your impact.	▪ Story and character development takes gifted individuals or teams. This is especially true when it comes to coming up with captivating subplots while also maintaining a good overall plot.
"How to" videos/ tutorials: These are videos which are designed to pass on skills or knowledge to viewers.	▪ More and more people learn new skills by watching videos as the combination of narration with moving images clarifies realities or processes that are hard to describe in words only. This is a great opportunity for serving the needs of marginalized communities. Creating tutorials in their language can allow even illiterate viewers to acquire new skills that can improve their well-being. ▪ Video tutorials can also be used to raise the status of a language or community by passing on local know-how.	▪ Requires presenting information and processes in a clear way, without making the video(s) too long.

(continued)

Video genre	Strengths	Challenges
Documentaries: As with audio documentaries, viewers are taken to one or more locations to discover reality for themselves. Video documentaries are powerful because you can use a "talking head" (see section 7.4) approach for your interviews and illustrate what is being shared with images. This can clarify realities and emotions that can be hard to transmit through audio interviews and sound effects.	<ul><li>They are captivating because viewers get to come along on a journey and discover things for themselves.</li><li>Because you are documenting reality through the eyes of people, viewers easily understand and identify with your topic. This demonstrates God's love in a holistic and tangible way.</li><li>The lack of vocabulary is less of a problem than with audio documentaries because realities that cannot be put into words can be presented visually.</li><li>Documentaries are great for awareness-raising or for exposing social sins by giving voice to people who are affected negatively.</li><li>Interviewees are usually more than ready to offer their services, as giving voice to them demonstrates genuine love and care and lets them be heard by others.</li><li>Documentaries can be used for advocacy purposes, fundraising or even reporting, to get outside partners involved.</li></ul>	<ul><li>Sometimes you will need to hide the face of interviewees and change their voice to protect them.</li><li>Some documentaries draw attention to issues that are politically dangerous.</li><li>Traveling to different locations, waiting for people to be available and shooting footage in public places can be time-consuming.</li></ul>
Event documentation: Events such as weddings, funerals, baptisms, Bible dedications, and other celebrations can be documented in video format using interviews and footage of key moments during the event.	<ul><li>Event documentations are very popular with viewers because they often hold great sentimental value to them. If you interview the right people using good questions, event documentaries give you an opportunity to combine factual storytelling with a spiritual component. Such videos can reach a wider audience.</li></ul>	<ul><li>It can be stressful to capture key events and interviews during the limited time an event offers you.</li><li>Some events take place in halls that are poorly lit, making it hard to get good images.</li></ul>

(continued)

Video genre	Strengths	Challenges
Reels: Reels are very short dynamic videos, lasting no longer than 60 seconds, created to capture the attention of social media users. The term was originally created for Instagram users.	• If using social media is the best way to connect with your target audience, reels allow you to regularly stimulate new conversations on your platform. Reels will often be shared many times by users, so if you include either a question or very brief message in your reels, packaged in a video everyone can relate to, this can create fruitful conversations. Imagine posting a funny 20-second reel on three ways to put on a mask for Covid-19 protection, ending the video with the statement, "Too bad masks don't protect our hearts!" What might happen? This may lead to a deeper conversation.	• If there are too many other reels that distract from your message, it can be hard to have a meaningful conversation.
Sign language Bibles/ Scripture portions	• For communities using sign languages, the Bible can be translated into video format in which the text is represented in sign language format.	• It is challenging to produce appropriate sign language Bible translations for all communities that need one, not least because of the many different sign languages spoken around the world and the lack of appropriate signs for Bible terminology in certain sign languages.

Having looked at a few of the most important video genres in Christian ministry, please remember this list is not complete, and there may be other formats which are worth considering. As you will have noticed, some of these video genres may be easier to use in your ministry context than others. We will now have a deeper look at video genres which can be contextualized more easily and are highly participative, as these are probably the most important audio genres to consider in most ministry contexts.

7.2 Image-based videos

7.2.1 Why?

Creating videos from still images has many benefits:

- Not only does it allow you to create videos without spending money on video recording equipment, the video editing process is often very simple and less time consuming than editing video clips, meaning you can put out more content within a given time frame.
- The simplicity of the process also means that building capacity in partners to create videos based on images is less time consuming and more sustainable than training partners in other forms of video production.
- Another advantage is that this approach leads to videos which give viewers the time to really absorb the images as opposed to having to follow the sometimes hectic flow of action in other types of videos. This creates a meditative atmosphere in which the audio of your video can also be fully absorbed. Videos using still images do not need to be boring. Using the Ken Burns effect makes it possible to animate images in such a way that the action that is visible on your images comes alive and feels progressive rather than static.
- Another reason for using still images in a video is that still images can often illustrate things you cannot record on film, either because you are covering past events or because you want to illustrate emotions or realities that cannot be made visible through video recording.

For this reason, videos based on still images allow you to create the following types of videos:
- ✓ Bible-story videos using Bible illustrations
- ✓ Videos using staged photos of Bible stories reenacted in contemporary life
- ✓ Simple documentaries
- ✓ Tutorial videos
- ✓ Event documentaries on past events for which pictures are available
- ✓ Simple videos using Bible texts followed by discussion questions

7.2.2 How?

Before you start a project, you will need to choose what type of still images to use. This might depend on what is available, but you may also decide to have a local artist contribute towards the project for more local buy-in. Another factor that influences your choice of images is whether to use photos or drawn illustrations. Here are some of the benefits for each of these options:

Photos are used to give your video an authentic look. Especially when photos are created in the context of your audience, this has the advantage that viewers can easily read the picture. Drawn illustrations, on the other hand, can be abstract and misleading

to some viewers. Using a photo approach means your video will easily stimulate your audience's imagination to make the story come alive to them, because the various visual elements in your video (clothes, buildings, backgrounds, body language, etc.) are very familiar to them. Photos also play an important role in video tutorials and documentaries that are made from still images. Because these video genres seek to transfer skills and knowledge about local realities, you will probably need photos that have been taken in the environment of your audience to illustrate different steps in a process or shed light on local realities.

Drawn illustrations (drawn or painted and then scanned) can illustrate information that is very difficult to capture in photography. You can use them to exaggerate emotions or show interesting perspectives to make a story come alive. You can also use illustrations to simplify complex realities to make them more understandable. Creating illustrations for a specific project requires a lot of effort and is highly time-consuming. So before you launch such a project, you will want to check online to see if you can find

suitable images that suit your purpose which you can use for free or for which you can obtain permission. Make sure you have a good idea of how many images you need for your project. You may find suitable images, but if the number of images is not sufficient, the amount of time spent on animating a single image will be too long and your video will become slow-moving and boring.

Another thing you need to keep in mind when looking for a set of images is to make sure your set covers the key elements of your video or story, otherwise a vital piece of visual information will be missing in your video. To solve this problem, look for a different set of images, but refrain from mixing image styles taken from different sets. This quick-fix approach will make your video look amateurish. One final thing about illustrations: To make sure your images are interpreted the way they need to be by your target audience, conduct a testing session in which you ask open questions about what your images represent.

When you have found the right collection of images for your video, remember that the quality of your video depends at least as much on the quality of your audio, as it depends on the quality of your images. Here is how you can **obtain great audio for your video**:

- Use a good quality sound card to record all of your narration and dramatization.
- Use different voices for different parts, either to dramatize or simply for diversification.
- Add background music and sound effects to make the setting and action come alive.
- Don't forget to record the title of your video or any slides with written text on them.
- Create a final audio mix for your video before you try to edit your video.

Once you have your images and audio ready, you can synchronize your audio mix with your images during **video editing**. There are many free video editors available online that allow you to create great videos using a few simple steps. Whatever software you choose, make sure it allows you to animate your images using the Ken Burns effect, change the duration of each image, add transitions between images and add titles to your project.

7.3 Music videos

7.3.1 Why?

Music videos are very powerful when it comes to reaching your viewers emotions. The way the lyrics of a song are repeated and embedded in a rhythmic and melodic sequence of moving images means audiences remember your message for a long time. Music videos allow you to mix different types of imagery. They allow you to mix imagery that highlight everyday experiences with images

of musicians performing a song. This creative mix of imagery lets the message of a song become even more tangible and memorable. Not surprisingly, secular and Christian artists alike use music videos to address social injustice or present their views on how the world can become a better place. Music videos also provide role models, as lead

singers and band members easily become heroes in the eyes of those who love their music, not least because they dare to speak out against deeply rooted social problems. The challenge for Christians is to know how to harness the incredible power of music videos for God's glory, and not for human glory. An important aspect of using music videos for God's glory is to create music videos with worship bands and choirs that already have a vision for using music for God's glory. Working with such groups will help you avoid promoting individual stardom. In many societies, being a member of a church choir is considered an expression of one's faith. In fact, being in a church choir is so popular that many churches around the world have several choirs, which take turns in leading the congregation in worship using different music styles. Creating music videos with church musicians is highly rewarding because it encourages your musicians to excel in their performance and lets them have an impact that goes beyond the boundaries of church services.

7.3.2 How?

In section 5.6, we saw that song composition is an important aspect of making sure music and music videos address current realities and issues. Without song writing, music videos may be seen as irrelevant by those in the general community. In addition to cultivating a practice of songwriting, here are a few practical steps to follow when creating music videos with church musicians:

- More often than not, individuals in a church choir or band will already have had some exposure to musical production, be it recording music or even creating a music video. However, in many cases, creating music videos will be something new and exciting for church musicians because of a lack of equipment or know-how within the church. Also, church leaders or musicians will often consider musical production to be too expensive or a waste of resources because they assume that it requires working with a professional studio or acquiring expensive equipment. The first step towards creating music videos with a church is therefore **breaking down false perceptions about the costs**. Offer your services to a church and let them discover that it is possible to create powerful music videos without expensive equipment.

- To create a first music video with a music group or church choir, ask them to choose a song they know very well and which can easily be performed in terms of body language. Sometimes choirs already have a repertoire of songs which they traditionally perform using extensive choreography, but it is enough if your musicians are able to move in a natural way to the beat of the song. Instead of trying to come up with a sophisticated choreography for their first music video, ask the musicians to pay careful attention to their facial expressions throughout the song, as these reflect most of the emotion and meaning of the song. Ask the musicians to practice the song well, as this will reduce the number of takes required during your audio and video recording sessions. It will also make sure your musicians are relaxed during the video recording, which in turn affects their facial expressions and body language.

- Before you prepare your video shoot, choose a location which takes into account the following factors:

  ✓ If possible, choose a place that has some **connection with the subject** of the song. For example, if you are making a music video about God's provision, why not record your video in a field during harvest time? Avoid using settings such as large villas with swimming pools, fancy cars or limousines in the background, which imply that the Christian faith is about material wealth. Instead, choose familiar settings that people recognize from their everyday lives. This lets your audience see that faith is a matter of ordinary everyday experience.
  ✓ Make sure there is **sufficient space** for the choreography and for positioning different cameras from different angles.
  ✓ Think about the **light conditions**: To have sufficient light on the faces of your musicians, the best locations are usually outside. However, you also need to think about the time of day. Choose a time of day during which there is no direct

sunlight blazing down on your musicians. Not only can the heat make the whole recording session unbearable for your musicians, it will also create shadows on their faces or lead to contrast problems with your camera settings. If there is no way around recording your video during the day, wait for a cloudy day or position your musicians in the shade, and make sure your background is about as bright as your musicians. Doing your video shoot in the morning or late afternoon is usually your best option if you want to use the direct sunlight. At this time of day, position your musicians in such a way that the sunlight illuminates them evenly from the front. However, filming too early or too late in the day is not ideal either because the rapidly changing light conditions will make it difficult for you to use images from different takes in your final edit.

✓ Choose a location with a **dark, neutral background**. Filming against a mountain, tree or forest, or even against a wall will make sure your musicians stand out against the background. If you want to further improve the contrast between your musicians and the background, consider asking the musicians to wear light clothes that stand out against the background.

- **Record your song before doing the video recording**. This allows you to use a playback of your final audio mix during the video recording, so that the musicians can perform the song in exactly the same rhythm as your audio. You can then synchronize your video recording with your audio mix during the editing process. This process allows your musicians to focus on the music during the audio recording, and on the visual performance and rhythm during the video recording. It also allows you to record the music in a quiet environment, as opposed to recording your audio outside during the video shoot where you cannot avoid the sounds of birds, cars, and other ambient noise. To read about how to record your music without needing a studio, see chapter 6.

- Once you have completed your audio edit, **prepare your video recording carefully**: Make sure you know where to position your cameras and what shot types and camera movements each camera should focus on. If you are using a **mobile phone** to record your video, you can use a single mobile phone but take three takes. Mobile phones do not have optical zooms, which means that to create a zoom effect you will need to move in and out (forward and backward) with your phone to get good images. To have a variety of angles for your edit, you can record a *wide shot* or *full shot* during Take 1, record *medium* to *medium close-ups* during Take 2 and move in close enough to get *medium close-up* to *extreme close-up shots* and *macros* during Take 3. If you are able to record your music video using **several cameras with optical zooms** (camcorders, DSLR cameras), I recommend positioning one centrally placed camera on a tripod and using two more dynamic cameras to the left and right of your musicians. This set-up will allow you to obtain a variety of angles and perspectives to make your music video interesting. In addition to using multiple cameras, I also recommend you record at least three takes of the performance. This way you will

have even more footage to choose from when you edit. What is more, this approach will help the performers to not feel all the pressure of a single recording as well as get used to having the camera around. Here is an example of how to record three takes of a music video using a three camera set-up:

Take Number:	**Camera 1**: On a stand in the center, facing musicians. Same position for all takes. No camera movement, no zooming.	**Camera 2 and 3**: Placed on sides, camera 2 on the left, camera 3 on the right. Some slow trucking (moving the camera sideways to the direction of the lens) or traveling in and out (camera moves in direction of camera lens).
Take 1:	Set to **wide shot** or **full shot**. This camera is used to create stable images to use where the other two cameras are shaky.	Careful zooming, from **full shots** to **medium close-up shots**.
Takes 2 and 3:		Careful zooming, from **medium close-up shots** to **extreme close-up shots** and **macros**.

- One more thing about your video recording: If you can add a high angle to your recording by using a drone or finding a different way of recording the video from above (climb a tree, use a balcony or wall), this will give a very different angle to your video, as well as making it feel more professional. Also, consider recording additional images to tell a story without words or show some realities from everyday

7.3 Music videos

life that connect with your song. Such images can really enhance the message of your music video.
- During editing, you can use images from all of your takes, as long as light conditions did not change drastically during the video recording session. When choosing your best clips, your final take will often give you the best images because your musicians are more relaxed. Make sure you create frequent transitions between different angles, as well as adding some interesting effects to your video such as slow-motion or cross-fading between different shots to enhance your video.

For **advice on video recording equipment and procedures**, read chapter 8.

7.4 "Talking head" videos

7.4.1 Why?

One of the most effective ways to create informational videos, documentaries, or how-to videos is to use a "talking head" approach. Rather than doing an audio recording of your narration and adding images to it, this approach uses video interviews to let others narrate your video by talking directly to your audience. This does not mean that, as a producer, you cannot be one of the talking heads yourself. However, letting others also present information in your video via a talking head approach has many benefits:

- This approach is far more engaging to your audience because of the nonverbal elements that become visible and because the information presented by the interviewees becomes more personal. It also makes it possible to include personal testimonies or examples to highlight the information that is being presented.
- You can give voice to people with real expertise or experience, rather than researching all of the information by yourself. As a result, your video will be much richer in terms of its educational value and more believable. In addition, giving voice to others allows you to encourage and empower ministry partners.
- If you were to script all of the narration yourself, your video might easily become overly factual or hard to follow. Using interviews, on the other hand, makes sure the information you present is easily understood, because interviewees usually respond using the kind of vocabulary and simple sentence structure that is found in everyday language.

- Video interviews allow your interviewees to visually demonstrate what they are talking about during the interview. An interviewee may, for example, lead you through an orphanage or pineapple plantation, pointing out various aspects of their project, while talking on camera. Similarly, if you are creating a tutorial video, your interviewee can demonstrate the various steps in the process live on camera, while narrating the process or responding to questions that will clarify the process to your audience. If such dynamic interviews are not feasible, you may still be able to conduct your interview in a location that relates to the topic. If this is the case, this allows you to record additional footage at the time of the interview to illustrate the information presented by your interviewee. Whatever approach you use, using an interview-based approach will make it easier to edit your video, and the resulting images will perfectly illustrate the information and processes that are presented.
- You can use this approach for addressing topics that are more personal in nature. Say you want to create a video about how a particular tradition negatively affects certain individuals in a community. If the target audience of your video is the affected community itself, your video should not focus only on presenting facts, but rather seek to speak to the hearts of your audience. In this instance, you will probably want to create a testimonial video, which allows those who are marginalized to share their stories and emotions.

To summarize, using a talking head approach is a highly effective method for creating a number of different informational or educational videos. Because of the versatility of this approach, this book does not cover similar genres such as documentaries or testimonial videos separately. Here are some examples of the kinds of videos you can create using the talking head approach:

- ✓ A video to present the objectives of an organization, project, or training event to its beneficiaries or potential partners.
- ✓ Event documentation videos (Bible dedications, training events, celebrations, opening of a new church, etc.)
- ✓ Creating tutorial videos to present or transmit knowledge or skills, for educational purposes, or to strengthen local identity (languages, culture, know-how).
- ✓ Videos for awareness-raising to protect marginalized people or mobilize support to help them.
- ✓ Testimonial videos that help personal faith become more tangible.

7.4.2 How?

Having a good idea of the structure of your video is probably the most important factor for creating effective talking head videos. Essentially, you want to make sure that each interview fits into an overall framework, which guides the information flow. One way of doing this is to divide your video into three main sections: An introduction, insights from one or more practitioners, followed by a closing and final information part. This structure will help you identify who to interview as well as what questions to ask for each section. Obviously, you do not need to interview other people for every section. It may, for example, make sense for you as the producer to present the introduction section yourself, or to present the conclusion section. In this case, your presentation may not feel like an interview, but you still want to speak to the camera as if your audience had asked you specific questions. Whatever you choose to do, the people that respond (or present) on camera must talk freely and more or less without interruption, while presenting information in a logical manner that takes into account what audiences might or might not already know. Here is an example of the kinds of questions your interviewees might respond to for each section, if you were to create a talking head video on moringa[23] cultivation and its benefits for your target audience:

Introduction	Practitioners	Closing: Summary and information
Who? Michel, owner of two moringa plantations and vendor of natural remedies, speaks the language of the target audience fluently.	**Who?** Three different moringa farmers with different levels of experience and different responsibilities on the farm, who all speak the language of the target audience.	**Who?** You yourself, the producer.
Questions: When did you plant your first moringa farm and what motivated you to do this? Can you give us an overview of the many benefits of moringa?	**Questions**: Can you show us how you harvest morgana leaves? How do you process the leaves and what will be the final product? What challenges do you face in managing this moringa farm?	**Questions**: What is your advice in terms of starting a moringa farm, be it from a practical point of view, as well as in terms of God's promises? How can we (viewers of this video) make use of moringa products for our health? What do these products cost, and how can we purchase them?

---

23 Moringa is a tree with many health benefits, as well as the potential for income generation and job creation.

When you conduct an interview, you want to make sure the response flows in such a way that it answers several questions in one go, without viewers having to hear the questions or you having to keep asking new questions. In other words, your interviewees should embed any information from your questions in their response so that the response makes sense by itself and can be used without requiring a lot of additional editing. Here is an example:

Question: *Do you have water for your trees throughout the year, or does the dry season mean your well dries up?*

Answer: *Well, that depends! Sometimes this does happen, but other times we manage to have water throughout the year (end of the response).*

In this example, your question has led to a response, which is practically useless for the purpose of your video, because you would have to include your question in the video, as well as having to ask another question to keep the answer going. Instead, you could ask the question:

Question: *Can you tell us a little bit about how you manage to water your plants throughout the year and what some of the challenges are that you face? Please just talk freely. Please start by saying,*
"One of the most important aspects of managing a moringa farm is..."

Answer: *One of the most important aspects of managing a moringa farm is making sure the trees are watered throughout the year. The way we do this is that we...*

Using such examples and coaching your interviewee in their response will help them speak more freely, while giving a response that has a logical build-up. One final piece of advice on interviews: To make your video even more appealing, you can add a **vox pop** section to your video. As discussed in section 5.9.2, this requires cutting short sections of responses from different people into an interesting mix of voices. To use our example of a talking head video on moringa farming, you could start the video with a short vox pop on what people on the streets know or don't know about moringa.

In addition to using the right structure and questions during your interviews, you will need to **record additional footage** to accompany your talking head video interviews. In the example graphic of a video interview, below, this footage is labelled "illustration". During the video editing phase of your project, your best and most appropriate sections of this footage will be placed above your interview clips so that you can keep hearing the audio of your interview, while seeing images that illustrate what is being said. This approach leads to engaging videos that hold your viewer's attention as different interviewees appear, disappear, and reappear on camera, with a variety of images appearing in between that illustrate what is being talked about. Here is an example of a final edit of a talking head video on moringa farming:

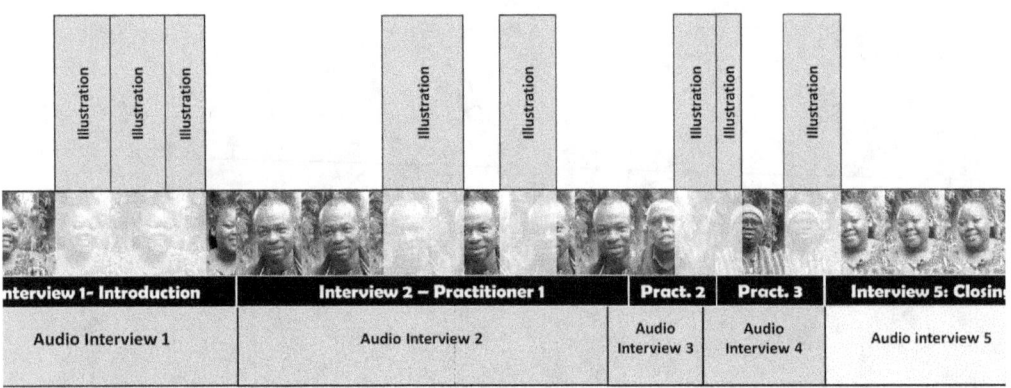

For more information about the technical process of recording interviews, please read chapter 8 on video recording equipment. However, it is worth mentioning here that **virtual meetings can be a great way of conducting interviews** with people who are busy or in a far-off location. For recordings via online meetings, make sure your interviewees are positioned in such a way that they are well illuminated and consider recording each person separately via a tie microphone, so that you can synchronize a higher resolution audio recording mix into the video recording of your interview.

7.5 Participatory short films

7.5.1 Why?

Traditionally, films are created by individual script writers and film directors with significant budgets, large film crews, and professional actors at their disposal. Using highly commercialized processes, the film industries around the world are able to put out great numbers of highly entertaining films and series to suit our seemingly insatiable hunger for entertainment. While there is much we can learn from professionals, we need not compare ourselves with them in terms of know-how, budgets, or available film crews and camera equipment. Participatory film-making offers a process that is unique. While the film industry tends to produce films for fame and money based on mainstream worldviews and the realities of large audiences, there are plenty of communities around the world whose realities and languages will never attract the attention of secular film industries. This is where creating Christian short films with audience participation has the following benefits:

- By participating in a film project, your audience can suggest topics and craft stories that are drawn from local realities and address real needs.
- Participatory film-making allows you to create films using local languages.
- Participants in film projects have a personal interest in sharing the film with others, as well as talking with others about the message of the film. This increases the impact of the film.
- Films can demonstrate the long-term outcome of the attitudes and behavior of different people, which in turn provides positive or negative role models to your viewers.
- Films allow you to show the imperfections of Christians, as well as demonstrating how the Holy Spirit is at work in ordinary life decisions. This gives your viewers a better understanding of God's work in us and through ordinary life experience.

7.5.2 How?

When developing a film for a given community, it is possible to write the script yourself and recruit actors for it. However, unless you have very good knowledge of the target community, your message and story can easily become superficial and unrealistic. Developing films based on choices made by your target audience and drawing from a number of testimonies of local participants will ensure your film becomes authentic. To do this, you can use the same participatory message and story development tool called HEARD described in section 5.5.2. The HEARD process will not only provide the insights and inspiration you need for a good plot and relevant message, but it will also result in more ownership for the film and good acting. When participants play a part in developing the characters of a film and appointing actors for different roles, it is amazing how easily your participants will identify with the characters of your film and how naturally they are able to act out their roles. Because the HEARD process is entirely oral, it allows participants of all ages and all educational backgrounds to take part. The difference between using the HEARD approach in radio drama and using it for film making, is that film making requires that you create a film script after you have developed your film story. When recording the audio of a radio drama, it is possible to improvise and improve the acting out of a scene using oral processes only. This is also the case for shooting the scenes of your film. Generally, you can let your actors improvise their dialogue and acting for each scene and repeat the scene after reviewing it to improve it. However, films require a clearer idea of where each actor will be placed, how they will move and how different cameras should be set up. For this reason, I recommend preparing a word-by-word script for each scene, which also includes how the different cameras are set up.

> **H**ear out heartfelt topics and testimonies.
>
> **E**ncourage endorsement.
>
> **A**gree on needed actors and action.
>
> **R**ecord, review and repeat improvisation until ready.
>
> **D**igitally edit for diffusion and dialogue.

Preparing a film script

Before we talk about how you can convert your film story into a film script, it is important to note that films rely heavily on allowing your viewers to follow the events of a scene from different angles. If you shoot an entire scene using only one camera and without changing your shot, your film will not hold your viewers' attention in the same way. This means that you need to understand basic shot types and camera

techniques before you shoot your film. While it is very possible to develop your film without writing a script (for example, using an oral participatory process) once your story is developed, deciding how to shoot each scene will require that you at least write up or draw the camera placements and shots you intend to use. In addition, it is recommended that you write a more detailed dialogue script for each scene. This script will not serve the purpose of allowing the actors to memorize their lines. Rather, they will help you as film director to have a good idea of what needs to be said concretely in each scene, so that you can guide the actors in their improvisation. Below is an example of a script for a film scene to give you an idea of the main components to include in a film script. You will see that the script uses abbreviations for the shot types that are assigned to different cameras, as well as simple illustrations to show how the subjects should appear on these shots. It is important to understand that film scenes are usually filmed using several cameras, with each recording the entire scene. During the editing phase you can then synchronize the video clips from all cameras with each other, before choosing which camera angle to show for specific time slots in the scene. Before we look at the script of Scene 1, here is how three cameras were set up for this shoot:

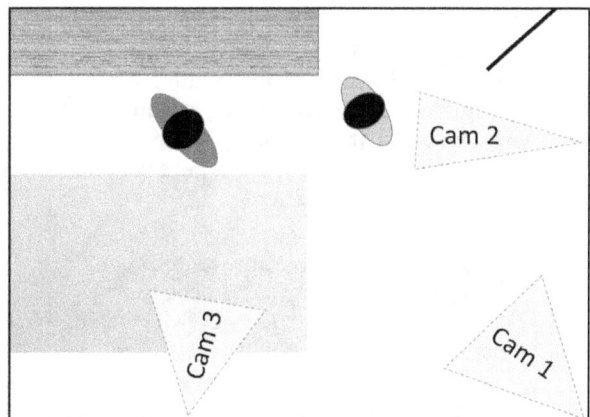

James and Mary are arguing in their bedroom about whether or not to give a bribe at a job interview, while James is getting dressed.

Camera 1 is on a tripod, records a Full Shot (FS) of the scene.

Cameras 2 and 3 capture the faces and gestures of the conversation, zooming between a Medium Close-Up Shot (MCU) and a Close-Up Shot (CU). Camera 2 focuses on James, camera 3 on Mary.

Dialogue and Description	Camera 1	Camera 2	Camera 3
Scene 1 J: *Shouts*: Honey..., what do you think? Should I wear this one, or this one? *Holds up options.*	FS	MCU–CU	MCU–CU
M: *Enters the room.* **I told you; I like the dark one better. It makes you look more like a teacher!**			
J: OK, then let me wear this one. *Fiddles with clothes in the cupboard.*			
M: **But as I told you, only looking nice won't help!**			
J: I know what you think my dear, but I told you, I'm not going down that road! *Concentrates on putting on dark shirt over T-shirt.*			
M: **Why not? Please, my love, we need the money! What about the kids? What about repainting the house, as you promised? Just think of it as showing them that you are the right person, that you are really motivated!**		Here, the camera operator of camera 3 is tasked to take a zoomed in Insert Shot of the envelope Mary tries to give to James. As you see, instructions in terms of specific shots to take can be added further down in this column, as the dialogue/ action unfolds.	I (Insert shot)
J: My dear, I don't have time to talk about this again. I'm already late, I need to leave! *Begins to leave.* Anyway, why would money show that I am motivated? And how would you feel working at a school when you have taken the place of someone else, maybe even someone who is better qualified? If God doesn't open this door, he will provide something better!			
M: *Laughs.* **Come on, even you know that that's not true! If you don't play their game, you will always miss out!**			
J: My dear, I really need to go! Please just pray! *Leans against doorpost.*			
M: **Of course, my dear, you know I will!** *Walks off in a hurry.*			

Directing your film: Directing a film means giving instructions to your actors and camera crew, so that recording your scene goes smoothly. For every scene, you will need to make sure that:

- There is enough light on the actors and action.
- There aren't any disturbing background noises that could ruin your recording.
- Your setting and actors are well prepared (decor, clothes, final instructions on acting, etc.)
- Your audio and video technicians have set up and tested their equipment, including making sure the equipment has sufficient battery life and memory to complete the shoot.
- Constructive feedback is given after each take and the take is repeated until the scene is well done.

7.5.3 Shot types and camera techniques

Framing your shot

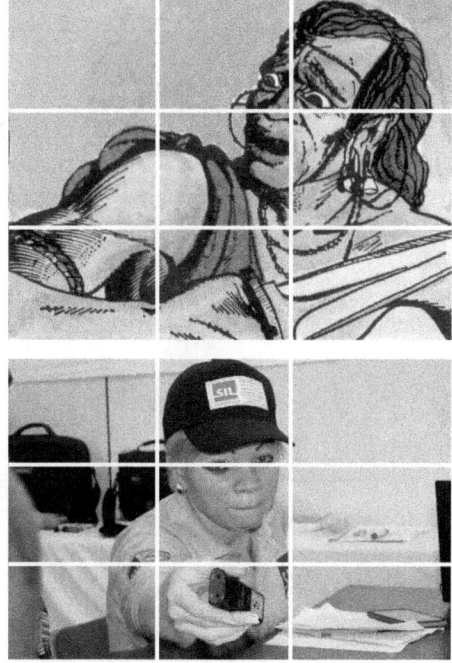

Although your camera allows you to capture images in any way you want, not all shot framing, perspectives, and changes in perspective are pleasant to the eye. Our eyes are used to reading (processing) what we see in a particular way, and as video producers, we must be aware of this and exploit it if we want to communicate successfully with our pictures. The Rule of Thirds describes the phenomenon according to which your main focus in a framed image should be placed on one of the lines that divide your image into thirds, if possible, at an intersection between two of them. This rule will always result in framing your image in a way that is pleasant and meaningful to the eye, regardless of whether your image is moving or not (photo, video, or drawing), whether it is in portrait or landscape format, and whatever the subject may be (people, countryside, or objects). The amount of space that is left towards the left or right of your point of focus, as well as above or below it, indicate the direction into which the main subject you have framed is looking or about to act. For example, the hunter with the knife is looking down to our left side, while the girl with the recorder is looking straight at us.

Shot types

To communicate the right emphasis throughout a scene, make sure you select an appropriate sequence of shots to tell your story. Below are all major shot types as well as their abbreviations for use in script writing. Essentially all shot types will fit in one of two main categories:

1. Shot types with regard to the setting:	
The **Extreme Wide Shot (EWS)** presents the scene in its overall setting:	The **Wide Shot (WS)** shows just the part of the setting that is important for the action:

2. Shot types with regard to people:	
The **Full Shot (FS)** shows the whole person while giving an idea of the setting:	The **Medium Long Shot (MLS)** cuts the person off around the knees:

(continued)

2. Shot types with regard to people:	
The **Medium Shot (MS)** cuts the person off at the waist: 	The **Medium Close-Up (MCU)** cuts the person off at the chest: 
The **Close-Up (CU)** Shot cuts the person off where the tie is knotted: 	The **Big Close-Up (BCU)** and **Extreme Close-Up (ECU)** Shots present details of the face, hands, feet, or other parts of the body:   Note: Close-ups of objects are sometimes also called Inserts (I) because these shots often need to be shot separately from the live action.

The **choice of shots** used in a scene will depend on what you want to communicate. For example, if the action takes place on a public street showing a man driving off quickly, excited to go visit a friend, you might an *Extreme Wide Shot* to show just how quickly he approaches the camera from a distance and disappears. However, to show the man's joy or excitement, you might use an additional *Close-Up* or *Big Close-Up* so that viewers can see his emotions, as he starts the engine.

Using different **angles** also convey meaning. When you use a **Low Angle (LA)**, you are looking up at the main subject, which presents them as being in a position of power or dominance. When you present your subject using a **High Angle (HA)**, this emphasizes their lack of power or insignificance. Sometimes the camera is placed in a way that shows the perspective of the subject, allowing the viewer to see what the subject sees. This is called a **Point-of-view shot (POV)**. Another way of showing what your main subject sees is called an **Over-the-shoulder shot (OTS)**. It will always include the shoulder of your main subject while showing the face of the person they are talking to. This creates a sense of intimacy and identification with the main subject. One more thing that is noteworthy is that you will often want to combine several angles and shot types in a single shot, either in the way a picture is framed or in the way your framing evolves over time.

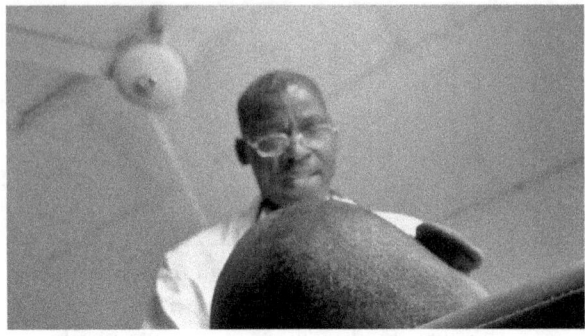

Low Angle:
> The doctor has the power to heal.

High Angle:
> This man has overcome the rough terrain, it lies subdued at his feet.

Point-of-view shot (also OTS):
> What have I done this time?

Camera techniques

In addition to how an image is framed, camera techniques help you convey by making progressive changes to what is being framed:

- **Zooming**: This refers to progressively changing the frame of your image using a camera's lens, making things appear closer or further away. Zooming in allows you to slowly draw the attention of viewers towards an element that is already visible to them, such as a person's face, while removing other elements from the frame. When zooming out, you can begin to let new elements appear in your frame, creating a sense of suspense (for example, by revealing the presence of another person in the room). Note: The more you zoom in on your image, the more important it is to stabilize your camera to avoid blurriness from camera movement. Zooming is different from forward tracking or backward tracking (moving the camera in and out in the direction of the lens), because when zooming, your camera position remains the same, while the way your background appears relative to the subject changes progressively.
- **Camera movements**: These are the most frequently used camera movements:
    - **During vertical panning**, also called **tilting (VP, T)**, the camera pivots on its vertical axis. When the camera tilts vertically, it films from top to bottom or bottom to top. In order to get an idea of vertical panning, simply stand upright and tilt your head from top to bottom or bottom to top.
    - **During horizontal panning (HP)**, the camera pivots on its horizontal axis from left to right or right to left. In order to get an idea of a horizontal panning shot, simply stand upright and turn your head from left to right or right to left.
    - When you are **tracking (Track FW, Track BW)**, the camera follows a person throughout the scene, either forward or backwards. To imagine the effect of this technique, simply walk forwards or backwards behind a person and change direction with them: you get the impression the world is slipping. This is what tracking looks like on the screen. A **dolly shot (D)** is similar in that the camera moves in and out of your action (dolly in and out), but you are not following a particular person. A **trucking (Truck)** shot also follows the action, but sideways, moving at a right angle to the filming direction.

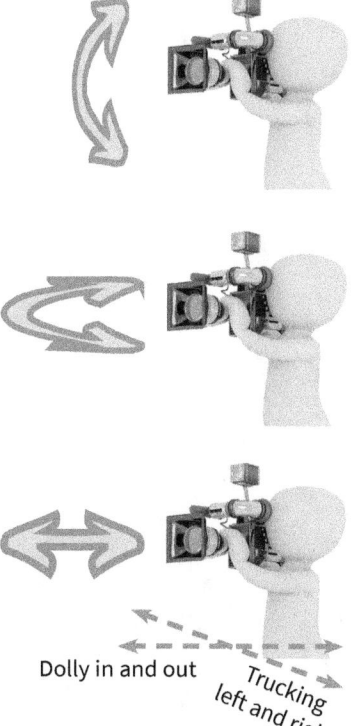

Dolly in and out

Trucking left and right

- **Subject movement**: Instead of moving the camera's shooting angle or the camera itself, you can also change a shot by letting a subject (person, vehicle, animal, etc.) join or leave the frame. For example, a Medium Close-Up shot of a character can suddenly change to a Full Shot of a second person standing in the background of your frame when the first person leaves the scene.
- **Focusing**: Another camera technique for making images more dynamic is focusing. This method is only possible if your camera has a powerful enough lens and manual focus. By using a low aperture (f-stop), you can bring only those parts of the picture into focus that have a certain distance to you, while everything that is closer or further away remains blurred. To create a sense of dynamic movement or reveal a new subject, simply change the focus point between the foreground and background.

8
Video Recording Equipment

With the many types of cameras available on the market, choosing the right equipment for your projects can seem overwhelming and confusing. Should you buy a camcorder, a DSLR camera (digital single lens reflex), a DSLM camera (digital single lens mirrorless), or might a small point and shoot camera or smart phone be enough for your projects? Let me start by saying that rather than making choices based on the cost of a camera, understanding what leads to good quality images will allow you to find affordable equipment that will give you great results. The following are some important points to consider when purchasing a camera:

1. **Picture quality and resolution:** The way cameras are often advertised is by promising higher image resolution than other models. However, this information is usually misleading, because this information usually tells you how much information the sensor of a camera can handle, regardless of whether the lens of your camera provides enough quality and detail to make use of the sensor's capacity. This is why it is always best to test a camera before you buy it, or look up reviews online. When a photo is enlarged, can you see enough details? Are the colors natural? Do not forget to also test the quality of videos, as there may be considerable differences between videos and photos with regard to picture resolution.

2. **Zooms:** Does the camera come with an optical lens that allows you to zoom in and out? What is the widest shooting angle and how close can you get to a subject? The greater the range between the widest and narrowest shooting angle, the more options you have for presenting the action in an interesting and varied way. Also, having a good zoom will

enable you to film more easily with two cameras, because you can stand outside the angle of shot of other cameras. Be careful, however, with digital zooms. These only give the impression of bringing the picture closer. In reality, they only digitally increase the size of the picture and you lose out in image quality. This is, for example, the case with most smart phone cameras.

3. **Screens**: Does the video camera have a screen? Whether it is large or small, if a screen is movable, it will enable you to take pictures from interesting angles without having to lie down on the ground and without having to keep your eye on the viewfinder, especially if you have a screen that can be rotated. Of course, screens use up a lot of battery, and they can be hard to see when shooting in direct sunlight, so it's best to have the option of turning it off. This is the case with DSLR / DSLM cameras and some camcorders that have viewfinders.

4. **Batteries and disk space**: One of the greatest problems with video recordings is that they usually take more time and space than is possible with a single battery or memory card. Most cameras come with special batteries, but it is worth looking into how many options there are in terms of alternative batteries in the current market, battery prices, and how likely it is that replacement batteries will be available in the future. It is probably a good idea to buy replacement batteries while they are still available on the market and go for a camera where batteries are likely to be available in the future. This also has the advantage that you won't run out of battery power in the middle of a project. Also ask yourself this: Would it be helpful to get a camera that uses regular batteries which can be bought anywhere? This will ensure you will never run into the problem of a lack of replacement batteries in the market. In terms of the amount of space you need, will you typically be recording a lot of footage while on a trip, or can you transfer your files regularly to a hard drive or computer? Internal memories on cameras are often larger than memory cards, but when they run out of space, they run out of space. Memory cards, on the other hand, don't take up much space and you can have several cards ready to replace a full card, but you will need to make sure you get cards that are compatible with your camera's shooting mode and image resolution.

5. **Audio recording**: Generally, cameras do not offer good audio recording capability. This is because most cameras contain poor quality microphones and poor quality sound cards. This means that you need to find ways to do a separate high quality audio recording while doing your video recording. However, it is still worth checking the quality of your camera's audio recording because it will serve as the basis for synchronizing your good quality audio recording with your video. Also, sometimes the audio recording of your camera can be a lifesaver when your separate audio

recording fails during an important recording. When comparing different camera options, look for the audio settings as well, as some settings such as noise reduction, filters that focus on voice frequencies, or even the option of changing the angle of sensitivity of your microphone to a more directional angle (shotgun or zoom microphone settings) can help you get a cleaner recording. Another thing to look for is a port for plugging in an external microphone. While your audio will still be affected by the quality of the camera's sound card, using a higher quality external microphone can improve your audio.

Comparing three major camera types: To summarize the key characteristics discussed above, here are the particular strengths of three major camera types:

Smart Phones	Camcorders	DSLR / DSLM cameras

<ul><li>Are very portable and discreet, which makes recording spontaneous interviews or other footage in public places easier and feel less threatening to those involved.</li><li>Smart phones have internal batteries that can last a long time and which can be charged easily via portable power banks.</li><li>Usually do not offer optical zoom.</li><li>The image quality is not always the best because of limited optics but some mobiles phones have exceptional video resolution and image quality is continuously being improved.</li></ul>	<ul><li>Camcorders have great focus capabilities, meaning they easily find and maintain the right focus point.</li><li>They often offer powerful optical zoom. However, beware of the digital zoom which sets in at some stage.</li><li>The zoom control buttons allow you to zoom in and out smoothly.</li><li>Most camcorders have movable screens.</li><li>You can find affordable camcorders with excellent image quality.</li><li>Camcorders usually have externally mounted batteries with good battery capacity.</li></ul>	<ul><li>DSLR and DSLM cameras have large and removable lenses. This allows you to get good images even in low light conditions and use an almost endless range of shooting angles if you have different lenses at your disposal.</li><li>DSLR cameras sometimes struggle with finding and keeping focus in dynamic video recording mode. DSLM cameras on the other side have very powerful focus technologies.</li><li>DSLM cameras offer slimmer camera bodies, often at the cost of reduced battery capacity.</li><li>Some lenses require manual zooming, which can create instability.</li><li>DSLR cameras tend to be more expensive.</li></ul>

Audio recording in videography: When recording audio for a video, you typically want to find a way to do recordings in dynamic situations or in a way that is discrete, so that your microphones are not visible on camera. Boom microphones, shotgun microphones or wireless microphones are all tools to consider if you want to get good results, but all of them are expensive. Thankfully, there is another solution that is much more affordable, while providing probably the best possible audio quality in video recording situations: By connecting a tie microphone (lapel microphone) to a portable recorder (or mobile phone), you can place your microphone on your subject in a way that your microphone is not visible (or at least hide the cables), while your subject can move about, carrying the portable recorder in their back pocket. This set-up can be used for recording dialogue when shooting a film, or for interviews. Tie microphones are generally very affordable, and even medium quality microphones offer excellent audio quality, if you know which ones to buy. If you don't have a portable recorder, you can try combining your tie microphone with a smart phone, as some smart phones have decent sound cards in them. Whatever your set-up may be, make sure your microphone has the right connector: TRRS (tip-ring-ring-sleeve) connectors are mini-jack connectors with 4 parts (3 divisions). TRS (tip-ring-sleeve) connectors are mini-jack connectors with 3 parts (2 divisions). TRRS connectors are used for plugging inputs that combine microphone input with audio output signals. TRS connectors are used for microphone-only inputs on devices that have a separate plug for the audio output. In addition, or instead of these plugs, some mobile phones have USB-C type ports or other types of specialized ports, so make sure you get the right microphone for the recording device you plan to use. You can also get adapters so that your microphone can be used on different devices.

Additional video recording equipment: In addition to finding the right camera or cameras for your projects, consider purchasing some of the following pieces of equipment:

- **Tripods**: It is hard to imagine doing any kind of video recording without the stability offered by tripods. Yes, there are techniques for holding your camera still, but tripods create absolute stability, and they set your hands free for other things, including operating another camera. For interesting perspectives or when traveling light, consider using a small flexible tripod that can be mounted to irregular surfaces. If this takes up too much space, or if you do a lot of on-camera presentations, why not use a selfie stick?

- **Drones:** There are some very affordable drones on the market that are small and stable in the air, and can record good quality video. Using a drone in your shoot allows you to add new perspectives and motion into your shots that can make your video look professional. Note: Make sure you conform to local regulations about using drones in countries where these exist.
- **Lights:** While you can avoid most light issues by recording videos outside, every now and then you will wish you had some lights to illuminate your scene or interviewee. Why not get a small portable light with adjustable power and color temperature?
- **Action cameras:** If you need to shoot under water or position your camera in a car, on a motorbike, or on a moving object to create an interesting perspective, action cameras have become quite affordable and usually come with all kinds of mounts. They also have a wide angle, meaning you can record in tight spaces without any of the action being left out.

9
Script Writing

9.1 General principles of script writing

Here are a few criteria that will help you develop good scripts, regardless of whether you are preparing an audio or video production:

A good script **helps audiences visualize important information**: How can what is seen or heard help audiences visualize what is being talked about? A good audio script will use sound effects, narration, and dialogue to describe things that are visible, while video scripts should make sure that whatever is heard is also accompanied by appropriate illustrations.

Good scripts will **stimulate the imagination of your audience**. Ask yourself the following question: How do I choose sound effects, narration, and images for my production which will tap into the rich bank of experiences stored in the mind of my viewers, so that my content can transport them into mental places and events that feel real to them?

To have more impact, your script should **create a conversational atmosphere between you and your audience.** In both audio and video scripts, you can include questions or comments that are directly addressed to your audience, or which they can strongly identify with. This will let them feel that you are aware of their presence, and that you want to interact with them because you value their point of view. In talking head videos, the whole point of the genre is to let viewers feel that you are talking to them. However, even in other video genres, actors or presenters will sometimes suddenly turn towards the camera to say something directly to the viewers. All of these elements make your audience feel important and help maintain their attention.

Contrary to written information, audiovisual content **needs to be processed and understood in real time**. Long sentences or complicated sentence structures reduce the chance of being understood or even listened to. Good script writing will use vocabulary and sentence structures that are easy to follow, or seek to provide some guidance to voice actors or presenters, while giving them the freedom to speak naturally using conversational language.

9.2 Four types of scripts

It is important to understand that there are different ways to script your content. While most people think of a script as a word-by-word representation of what needs to be said, there are ways to script your content that will give actors and presenters more freedom to speak. This will result in a more natural and heartfelt language. Here are four types of scripts to consider, each with its particular strengths:

A) Word-by-Word scripts　　C) Content scripts
B) Key Expressions scripts　　D) Mixed scripts

A) Word-by-Word script

In a word-by-word script, every word is written and the recording and production follows exactly what was prepared in the script. At times, such scripts also prescribe what effects to use, when to use them, and the way one line or another should be acted out.

Word-by-word script

The Monkey in the Lion's Skin (10 minutes)
Written and told by Andreas Ernst, based on the original tale written by Dr. Paul White.

(*Forest sounds...*) Once upon a time, a little monkey called Toto was taking a nap in the middle of the forest. He was stretching out in his favorite tree, on his favorite branch. He was in a good mood. His eyes shone and a wide smile spread across his face from one side to the other: "Ah, how nice it would be to be a lion" (*with great satisfaction*), he thought. "I would be magnificent and handsome, powerful and respected by everyone. I would be the king of the animals." Feeling very satisfied with this image of himself, Toto stretched out on his branch to have a little midday snooze.
However, it was all just a beautiful dream! In reality...

Strengths:

- You can carefully craft your language.
- Your voice actors can memorize their lines in advance.
- You can make sure the dialogue or presentation provides the right information at the right time in complex productions such as film plots, tutorial videos, or documentaries.
- The recording can be made quickly if the reader or readers have prepared their text well.

Challenges:

- Texts that are read or memorized often lack the emotion and authenticity of natural speech.
- Written texts often use more complex sentence structures and vocabulary, which can make your content hard to follow.
- In some contexts, it is hard to find actors and presenters who can read.

B) Key Expressions script

This kind of script is made up of **key words and expressions**. These expressions help the speaker use specific, carefully chosen expressions, while freely adding their own natural words and expressions to embed them in.

Strengths:

- The speakers will use carefully chosen words and expressions, while also speaking naturally. This means you can, for example, make sure the right terminologies are used by different people in a consistent way, while ensuring the message feels authentic and is easily understood.

Challenges:

- Using specific phrases that may not feel natural, while speaking naturally, can be tricky. It takes quite a bit of practice and good reading skills.

Key Expressions script

<u>The Monkey in the Lion's Skin</u>

Once upon a time
taking a nap in the middle of the forest
favourite tree, favourite branch
wide smile across his face
king of the animals
respected by everyone
not in the least magnificent
however didn't look much like a king
just between you and me
not even a village chief
day and night, leftovers of avocados
huge pile of rotten fruit
in spite of this, wasn't about to drop the idea
one day, by sheer coincidence…

C) Content script

To let your presenter or actor speak freely from their mind and heart, you can use a content script. A content script is essentially a list of points that need to be covered during the recording. These points can be the steps in a story, as with the example below, or bits of information or arguments that need to be highlighted. The content script does not prescribe any of the language that needs to be used to communicate the content. In fact, in some cases, you do not even have to follow the order of the points listed in the script.

Strengths:

- Your actor or presenter will use expressive language that follows oral communication patterns. As a result, your audience will easily understand the content and follow with greater interest. Even the errors, repetitions, and pauses in the spoken word contribute towards a more interesting message.
- The different points in the script make sure important information is not forgotten and is presented in a logical order.

> **Content script**
>
> **The Monkey in the Lion's Skin**
>
> 1. Title and information about the origin of the text
> 2. Toto is having a rest
> 3. Toto would like to be a lion
> 4. Toto's real nature
> 5. Theft of a lion's skin
> ...

Challenges:

- The content must be understood and internalized.
- Your presenters/actors must have good oral communication skills.

D) **Mixed script**

To combine the benefits of the word-by-word script, the key expressions script and the content script, you can use a mixed script. Here is an example:

Mixed script

The Monkey in the Lion's Skin

Written and told by Andreas Ernst, based on the original tale by Dr. Paul White.

(Sounds of the forest …)

Toto is resting: stretching out, favorite tree, favorite branch

Toto would like to be a lion: how nice it would be, respected by everyone

Toto's true nature: not at all magnificent, didn't particularly look like a king, just between you and me: not even a village chief, wasn't about to drop the idea

Theft of the lion's skin: one day, by sheer coincidence …

9.3 Researching information for a script

As seen earlier, giving voice to people with expert insight and knowledge or drawing on the testimony of people with unique personal experience can add much educational value to your content. However, sometimes you as a facilitator or producer will need to acquire a deeper understanding of an issue you are covering to enrich your content. As you browse the internet or read up on a topic, here are a few principles to consider:

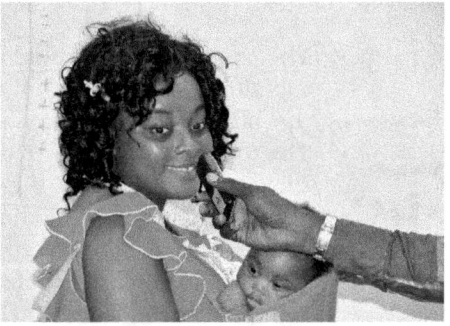

- Remember that information you do not understand yourself is not likely going to make sense to your audience. Avoid simply copying information and facts from books and websites, without checking it against other sources to make sure the information is reliable. Also, avoid using the style of language found used in texts, as this is usually hard to for audiences process. For example, avoid presenting scientific information using scientific terminology your audience does not understand.
- Make sure you are more interested in offering content that is useful from a practical point of view, as opposed to simply communicating facts or information. For example, telling your audience about the biological or chemical processes that are involved when they consume too much alcohol may not be very helpful. If, on the

other hand, you present concrete information about the damage alcohol can cause to their bodies, and then let people share personal testimonies about how alcohol reduced their health and how this affected their lives (memory loss, unemployment, loss of relationships, etc.), your content will offer real help.

- Presenting biblical advice: Bible commentaries and cross-references in your Bible allow you to draw up a list of passages that speak about a given subject. Studying and comparing such passages will help you have an overall view of the biblical view on an issue and not fall into the trap of responding to a particular problem in a superficial or erroneous way. For example, if you are looking for biblical teaching on the topic of adultery, do not only cover verses that condemn this behavior. Most people already know that adultery is immoral. Your content should also offer biblical advice on concrete aspects of the issue such as, for example:

- ✓ **The source of the problem**: Envy, selfishness, lack of discipline, a heart not submitted to God, a lack of emotional and physical intimacy between spouses, the influence of media, seductive behavior and clothing styles, pornography.
- ✓ **The consequences of the problem**: Hatred and unforgiveness between spouses, destruction of the family, lack of depth in the marriage, loss of faith or of responsibilities in church, a tendency to want to escape to yet another relationship that is more appealing.
- ✓ **The solution to the problem**: Submission to God and to each other, improved communication, forgiveness, understanding biblical advice on sexuality, understanding the supreme picture of marriage—God's covenant-like, long-term commitment to the church.

9.4   Intellectual property and copyright

By default, the copyright for an audio or video recording is held by the person doing the recording. However, this right is only valid if the people involved have given their consent for their voice and image to be used by the recordist for whatever purpose it is intended for. This means that it is a good idea to acquire the formal consent of any presenters, narrators, or actors in your production, for the way the recording will be used later. This is the case even if someone has only played a very small role such as reading a single line or briefly appearing in the background of one image.

In the context of Christian ministry, we easily assume that everyone has the same vision and sense of sacrificial service for the good of others. However, particularly when it comes to participatory communication, all kinds of people will get involved in your production, and chances are that eventually someone will complain about how their voice or image is being used, if for no other reason than to gain some form of financial benefit. This should not be your main motivation for respecting the law, so no matter what situation you are in, please obtain official written consent from any participants whose voice or image you are using in your production. For people who are nonliterate, you can obtain permissions via fingerprints or voice recording. In addition to listing all actors (voice or video) correctly by full name in your consent form, it is also a good idea to give some form of reward (financial or other such as a meal, travel expenses, gifts, etc.) to every contributing person. This is good practice anyway as it shows respect for the services of others. In addition, this practice can reduce the risk of being accused of having exploited others in order to complete a project. In addition to using the recorded voice or image of participants, you must also be sure to obtain permission for any AI-generated adaptations which you may want to create from your recordings.

Here is an example of a consent form:

Consent form

With my signature below, I allow _____ (name of organization) to use any recording of my voice or image, be it in audio or video format, for creating educational audiovisual content and distributing this content for noncommercial (and commercial) purposes. My permission includes the use of use of AI (artificial intelligence), with the agreement that AI will not be used to create any messages or false representations of myself which go beyond the scope of this current project. I also acknowledge having been remunerated for my service as described below:

Name:	Remuneration:	Date:	Signature:

As you share your content using appropriate media channels, make sure you **add the right Creative Commons license (CC)** to it. Creative common licenses allow you as the copyright holder to define how your content can be used by others, such as obliging others to give attribution when sharing your content, or making sure the content cannot be changed or used for commercial profit. However, be careful that you yourself do not violate any CC licenses.[24] If your content uses sound effects or images you have downloaded from the internet, or includes text or photos that are the creation of someone else, even if you have permission to use these resources, there may be a CC license on them that requires you to give attribution for them or limit the way you are able to modify or share these resources as part of your content.

---

24 https://creativecommons.org/share-your-work/cclicenses/

10
Conclusion

I hope this book has helped you appreciate the benefits of creating content that builds on the media habits and interests of audiences and involves them and key partners in all aspects of a given media initiative. Such participatory communication approaches allow us to work closely with target audiences and partners, which in turn makes it possible to build capacity in them to increase the impact and sustainability of media initiatives. Working closely with our target audiences also lets us first understand the needs and media habits of our audiences, so that we can identify the right media platforms and audiovisual content to reach them effectively.

Let me conclude by observing that one of the most important aspects of effective communication, besides interactivity, is continuity. This means that, in addition to methodological questions, we must also be aware of organizational factors that either favor or hinder using media as a regular communication tool for people with people. While I hope this book provides insight into why creating content for effective participation and communication is important and how to do it, methodology alone will not bring about the change that is needed to make use of the full potential of media for reaching people. Sadly, the structures and decision-making processes of some Christian ministry organizations fail to establish media services that are ongoing and embedded in the lives and habits of the very people they serve.

One major reason for this is that many Christian ministries are built on the concept of measurable, statistical impact. We like to measure our success by the number of Bible verses we have translated, books we have published, audiovisual products we have created, or even followers that have subscribed to a Facebook page. However, while accountability and reporting on measurable outcomes is important, translating the Scriptures into media is not an exact and measurable science. Investing in partnerships with existing media platforms or individuals who may or may not use the acquired media skills for years to come can be discouraging. In fact, it can be surprisingly difficult to obtain funding for such activities or dedicate staff to them. This can happen when funders want implementers to define measurable short-term outcomes or when there needs to be evidence of progress even in intermediate reports. However, investing in community-driven communication is a long-term goal, which requires building strong and sustainable relationships and networks with people through trial-and-error processes in order to gain long-term momentum.

Another reason why Christian organizations often fail to establish meaningful media services to reach the people they serve has to do with quality-control mechanisms. When creating content with people for people for ongoing needs, quality-control mechanisms cannot be guaranteed, nor should they occupy a central role in what we do. There are of course exceptions, such as quality-control mechanisms in dubbing biblical films or other production processes where content must closely match the expectations of copyright holders and ensure the product communicates accurately across cultural boundaries. However, such quality-control mechanisms cannot possibly be the norm when it comes to creating media content for the daily needs of our audiences. As organizations, we must recognize that staying in control of production-quality processes can become a hindrance to equipping and setting partners free for the gigantic task of creating context-specific content with people for people. Such content requires creativity and continuity, if we want to establish meaningful communication services that connect with people in the media environments that have become a daily refuge for almost every human being on this planet. It also requires trust and humility, as we let go of control and learn from the media experience of others or allow ourselves to depend on their services. Rather than focusing on audiovisual products and technologies, are we ready to overthrow some of our mental barriers and untangle our organizational blockages so that we can invest the time, money and personal comittment to long-term relationships that are needed to mediate God's Word into ordinary life experience through the voices of ordinary people?

Glossary

Begging the claim An argument in which the premises assume the conclusion without supporting it.

Hasty generalization An argument made based on a rushed conclusion without considering or offering enough evidence.

Ken Burns effect A panning and zooming effect over still images, used in film and video production.

Lectio divina A traditional practice of meditative scriptural reading.

Line A sentence or paragraph that is performed by a single voice actor, corresponds to a code in the script and is exported as a single sound file.

Plosive Also called 'pops': These are consonant sounds produced with the airstream completely blocked (for example 't', 'k', 'p'). When they are released, there is a sudden blast of air hitting the microphone.

Slippery slope An argument used to suggest negative consequences will result from an opponent's view or argumentation.

Straw man An argument used to misrepresent, exaggerate, or distort an opponent's argument to make it easier to attack.

References

Bessenecker, S.A. 2014. *Overturning Tables: Freeing Missions from the Christian-Industrial Complex.* Downers Grove, USA: IVP Books.

Campbell, Julia. 2020. *How to build and mobilize a social media community for your nonprofit in 90 days.* Bold and Bright Media.

De Campos Guimarães, J. P. 2009. Participatory approaches to rural development and rural poverty alleviation. In *Emerging issues in rural poverty reduction: The role of participatory approaches*, De Hague, Netherlands: Institute of Social Studies. https://sergiorosendo.pbworks.com/f/Guimaraes+2010+participatory_rural.pdf (Accessed 20 May 2024).

Dye, T. Wayne. 2009. The eight conditions of Scripture engagement: Social and cultural factors necessary for vernacular Bible translation to achieve maximum effect. *International Journal of Frontier Missiology* 26(2):89–98. https://ijfm.dreamhosters.com/PDFs_IJFM/26_2_PDFs/89-98_Eight%20Conditions.pdf. (Accessed 5 June 2025).

Erlacher, Jolene Cassellius. 2018. *Daniel generation: Godly leadership in an ungodly culture.* Virgil Press.

Ernst, A. 2016. Voices in action: What is the potential of participatory radio drama for empowering rural communities in Cameroon? MA thesis. Gloucester, UK: University of Gloucestershire. https://www.sil.org/resources/archives/79775 (Accessed 22 May 2024).

Ernst, A. 2021. *Participatory radio drama: Helping communities understand and share God's love through ordinary life experience.* Yaoundé, Cameroon: SIL International.

Jones, Nona 2020. *From social media to social ministry: A guide to digital discipleship.* Zondervan.

Lennox, John C. 2020. *2084: Artificial intelligence and the future of humanity.* Zondervan.

Lennox, John C. 2024. *Friend of God: The Inspiration of Abraham in an Age of Doubt.* 1st edition. La Vergne: SPCK Publishing.

Lie, R., and A. Mandler. 2009. *Video in development: Filming for rural change.* Wageningen and Rome: CTA and FAO.

Merz, J. 2023. Bible transmediation in theory and practice, *The Bible Translator* 74, 213–230. https://doi.org/10.1177/20516770221150806.

Myers, Bryant L. 2011. *Walking with the poor: Principles and practices of transformational development.* Revised and expanded edition. Orbis Books.

Parris, Matthew. 2008. As an atheist, I truly believe Africa needs God. *The Times* (UK), December 27, 2008. Cited in J. C. Lennox. 2024. *Friend of God: The inspiration of Abraham in an age of doubt,* 114. First edition. SPCK.

Peterson, Eugene H. 2006. *Eat this book: A conversation in the art of spiritual reading.* Eerdmans.

Picard, R. G. 2000. *Measuring media content, quality, and diversity: Approaches and issues in content research.* Turku, Finland: Media Economics, Content and Diversity Project and Media Group, Business Research and Development Centre, Turku School of Economics and Business Administration. http://www.robertpicard.net/files/Measuring_Media_Content_Quality_Diversity_Book.pdf (Accessed 30 August 2023).

Rogers, Everett M. 2010. *Diffusion of innovations,* Fourth edition. Free Press. https://books.google.hu/books?id=v1ii4QsB7jIC.

Servaes, Jan and Patchanee Malikhao. 2007. *Communication and sustainable development: Selected papers from the 9th UN roundtable on communication for development.* Rome: FAO. https://www.fao.org/3/a1476e/a1476e00.pdf.

Vokes, Richard. 2017. *Media and development.* Taylor and Francis.

Other Resources

Corbett, S., and B. Fikkert. 2012. *When helping hurts: Alleviating poverty without hurting the poor ... and yourself.* Moody Publishers.

De Fossard, E. 1996. *How to write a radio serial drama for social development: A script writer's manual.* Baltimore, MD: Population Communications Services.

Ernst, A. 2021. *Digital dialogue: Daring to stay relevant in an era of information overload.* Yaoundé, Cameroon: SIL International.

Ernst, A. 2023. *Eyes for impact: Visualized assessment and planning for effective Scripture impact.* youtube.com/watch?v=sr0_rjvkJ5I.

FAO-Dimitra. 2011. Community listeners' clubs: Stepping stones for action in rural areas. Brussels, Belgium: FAO. http://www.fao.org/docrep/014/am604e/am604e.pdf.

Henrich, D. J. 2003a. Education entertainment programming. In D. J. Henrich (ed.), *Mediastrategy and Christian witness: A special reader on media in the developing world,* 81–84. Handclasp International.

Henrich, D. J. 2003b. Participatory message development. In D. J. Henrich (ed.), *Mediastrategy and Christian witness: A special reader on media in the developing world*, 32–34. Handclasp International.

Hill, H., and M. Hill. 2011. *Translating the Bible into action: How the Bible can be relevant in all languages and cultures.* Piquant Editions.

Ilboudo, J. P. 2003. After 50 years: The role and use of rural radio in Africa. In Bruce Girard (ed.), *The one to watch: Radio, new ICTs and interactivity*, 199–210. Rome: FAO.

Lunch, C., and N. Lunch. 2006. *Insights into participatory video: A handbook for the field.* InsightShare.

Offor, J. O. 2002. *Community radio and its influence in the society: The case of Enugu State, Nigeria.* Frankfurt am Main: IKO-Verlag für Interkulturelle Kommunikation.

Ruggiero, T. 2000. Uses and gratifications theory in the 21st century. *Mass Communication and Society* 3:3–37.

Sposato, S., and W. A. Smith. 2005. *Radio: A post nine-eleven strategy for reaching the world's poor.* University Press of America.

Tacchi, J., and J. Watkins. 2008. Finding a voice through content creation. In J. Tacchi and J. Watkins (eds.), *Participatory content creation for development: Principles and practices*, 13–20. New Delhi: UNESCO.

Wendland, E. 2005. *Sewero! Christian drama and the drama of Christianity in Africa: On the genesis and genius of Chinyanja radio plays in Malawi with special reference to TransWorldRadio and African traditional religion.* Kachere Monograph 21. Zomba, Malawi: Kachere Series.

SIL Global

Publications in Scripture Engagement Series

ISSN 2994-7286

2. **Language in the Mission of God**, edited by Michael Greed, 2025, 290 pp., ISBN 978-1-55671-580-8 (pbk), ISBN 978-1-55671-581-5 (ePub).

1. **Translating the Bible into Media**, by Andreas Ernst, 2023, 94 pp., ISBN 978-1-55671-546-4 (pbk), ISBN 978-1-55671-547-1 (ePub).

SIL Global Publishing Services
7500 W Camp Wisdom Road
Dallas, Texas 75236-5629 USA
publications@sil.org

Andreas Ernst is a media and Scripture engagement consultant and SIL Global's Media Services' Director of Training and Equipping. He grew up in Cameroon, where his parents served in Bible translation. After studying pedagogy in Switzerland, he worked as a primary school teacher for a few years, before returning to Cameroon to serve with SIL in rural literacy and Scripture engagement projects. Ernst later studied contextualized theology at Redcliffe College in the United Kingdom and in 2016 earned an MA in Literacy Program Development from Gloucestershire University.

Besides serving as a language program manager, Ernst's professional experience has included heading up SIL's Francophone iDELTA training program (Institut pour le Développement des Langues et de la Traduction en Afrique), setting up community-owned radio stations, and developing media courses for SIL Global staff and ministry partners. He longs to see the integration of local languages and Scripture engagement in radio communication, social media and other media platforms that connect with the media habits of language communities. And he is passionate about participatory entertainment-education formations which allow audiences to connect the Christian faith to their every day lives.

His research interests include adult education, media ownership and entertainment-education genres that draw on people's testimonies to make the Scriptures come alive through ordinary life experiences.

Photo credit Eszter Ernst-Kurdi

Recent publications

(with E. Ernst-Kurdi) How Local Language Development and Community Radio are strengthening the Persecuted Church in Northern Cameroon, 2024. In J. Kaló, F. Petruska, and Lóránd Ujházi (eds.), *Budapest Report on Christian Persecution 2022-2024*. Budapest: L'Harmattan Kiadó, 260–270.

Eyes for Impact: Visualized, Participatory Planning and Assessment in Cross-Cultural Ministry. Paper presented at the Eighth International Language Assessment Conference (ILAC-8), 18–25 September 2024, Penang, Malaysia. https://www.audiovideoimpact.org/en/resources/eyes-4-impact-user-manual.

Quality in Media: Technical Excellence or Meaningful Engagement? Paper presented at the Bible Translation Conference, Dallas, TX, October 13–17, 2023. https://btconference.org/2023-proceedings/quality-in-digital-media-content-creation-can-communication-and-quality-checking-coexist?rq=ernst.

Eyes For Impact: Visualized Assessment and Planning for Effective Scripture Impact. 2023. youtube.com/watch?v=sr0_rjvkJ5I.

Participatory Radio Drama: Helping Communities Understand and Share God's Love Through Ordinary Life Experience (Course Manual). 2022. Translated from French by M. Lawson and A. Ernst. SIL International.

Digital Dialogue: Daring To Stay Relevant in an Era of Information Overload. 2021. SIL Cameroon.

Participatory Radio Drama. 2020. International Media News 106. SIL International Media Services.

Le Théâtre Radiophonique Participatif: La communauté s'exprime sur ses réalités pour rencontrer Dieu au quotidien (Manuel pour Facilitateurs). 2019. SIL Cameroun.

Audio Dramas for Scripture Engagement: A Participatory Oral Approach. 2018. SIL Cameroon.

Voices in action: What is the potential of participatory radio drama for empowering rural communities in Cameroon? 2016. MA thesis. Gloucester, UK: University of Gloucestershire.

Works by this author in SIL Language & Culture Archives

sil.org/resources/search/contributor/ernst-andreas